BECOMING A SUCCESSFUL INTERNATIONAL TEACHER

BECOMING A SUCCESSFUL INTERNATIONAL TEACHER

A concise step-by-step guide to international teaching

JESS GOSLING

Gosling DLA Press
Becoming a Successful International Teacher
Jess Gosling
jessgoslingearlyyearsteacher.com

Cover Design: GetCovers.com

First Published July 2021 by
Gosling DLA Press

Dedicated to my husband and partner in crime, for joining me on this journey abroad without question and to my daughter, for making me want to do better. Also dedicated to inspiring colleagues and managers who helped me love my career again.

Contents

PREFACE

For anyone who is considering a move abroad, the idea is both exciting and daunting. There are always a huge number of factors to consider. For someone who is a teacher, these concerns are amplified. Not only will they be moving to a new country, but they will have to navigate new ways of teaching, parent expectations, and language barriers within their classrooms. However, ask an international teacher whether they are happy that they made the move and they will invariably say 'Yes!'

This guide assumes that you are considering making a change in your career trajectory, from being a qualified teacher in your home country (with an internationally-recognised qualification gained in or from the UK, or with an equivalent qualification such as a US State License) to being a teacher working abroad.

I hope to support you on this journey. You do not need to do this 'blind', as this book will offer you all the guidance you need. My guide does not refer to theories or speak in detail about 'culture shock', 'assimilation', or other factors which are part of being an expat, but rather focuses on how to find a job, how to settle, and how to make a success of your placement abroad. I believe that the rewards of living and working abroad as a teacher are great and I wish I had had a guide to support me at the beginning of my journey as an international teacher.

I therefore decided to write this guide, as I saw a gap in the literature concerning *how* to become an international teacher written by an international teacher 'in the trenches' so to speak. I had only come across web pages and blogs, either written by recruiters or teachers.

Whilst this information was helpful, it lacked the depth required to really walk teachers through the steps on finding an international job and share insider's knowledge on both contacts and the process. Furthermore, I did not find any text that discussed what to do once you arrived and what would help you stay put! I know both the benefits and pitfalls as I have lived through many of them.

I want to support others, as working internationally has been the best career move I have ever made. When working in the UK over ten years ago as a primary teacher, I felt suffocated by the demands of the ever-expanding workload, pressures of the school, and the overall stress of working in a very challenging environment, for many reasons. Spending this time within the UK state school system helped me solidify my resolve to work internationally.

Fast forward 12 years and I have lived and taught in four countries. I have had an excellent quality of life in each place and have travelled extensively, enjoying luxurious holidays in places I would have only dreamed of prior to my move. I have experienced safaris in Africa, tracking orangutans in Borneo, theme parks in the US, interrailing around Europe, hiking in Thailand, and lazing on beaches in Vietnam. I have made life-long friends from around the world and my daughter has had an excellent, private education. I have also made a lump sum towards retirement and I continue to save. But most importantly, I have job satisfaction. I enjoy going to work each day, as I teach in a workplace where I have supportive colleagues and parents plus fantastic, motivated children.

I began this endeavour in order to support others to make this transition by creating a webpage and a short blog which discussed the key considerations for embarking on an international career. As I continued to add to my webpage, I realised there were some areas in which I had no experience, such as using paid recruitment agencies. I also recognised that only my voice was represented through the webpage. In addition to these considerations, I felt that the level of detail required to fully explain my journey into the international teaching world necessitated a larger publication rather than merely blog entries. Therefore, I decided that I would create a 'how to' guide and I would authenticate my work where necessary with the voices of other teachers, managers, and recruiters. This way, my research would reflect a broader spectrum of diverse voices (for an account of the research methods, see Appendix A).

Threaded through the guide is my own personal experience and opinion. It was important to me that my story was told within this book, to illustrate my life experiences and to offer encouragement. I hope the guide supports teachers to have the courage to take the first wonderful step and thrive in the international world of teaching. But remember, share this book with all those involved in your journey, such as your partner and children, so they are fully informed of what to expect.

I am always happy to receive questions and any further suggestions for this publication via the contact section on my website, jessgoslingearlyyearsteacher.com or my free Facebook group, New to International School Teachers.

Jess Gosling, 2021

CHAPTER 1

The Journey Begins

Will I be comfortable working abroad?

This is an important consideration. Most schools offer initial contracts of two years, which provide the opportunity to try the move short-term. There are also some opportunities to 'substitute' teach for an even shorter term within an international school, through companies such as 'True Teaching', aptly named the 'Flying Squad'. However, a move abroad can be very unsettling if you are not prepared. It is important to reflect upon whether you would 'fit' in this kind of lifestyle, especially the challenge of moving away from all that is familiar.

A recent study by Maria Savva found that international teachers had often enjoyed travel in childhood and the feeling of being immersed in another culture (22). The study also found that 'pivotal events' in the teacher's adulthood, such as studying or visiting friends abroad, had contributed to their desire to relocate. Consider if your past experiences would support such a move; for example, whether you have previously spent extended periods away from home in a culture different to your own.

If 'adventure' is the reason you wish to move abroad, you are not alone. Savva's study indicated that educators often communicated feelings of stagnation and frustration with their personal and/or professional circumstances when they decided to teach abroad. There are numerous advantages to such a move; these include a potentially better standard of living compared to home, travel and adventure, cultural enrichment, and the excitement of working within different types of schools and experiencing a different curriculum. Teaching positions abroad can offer excellent saving opportunities and the ability to advance your career at a faster pace than at home. Further, if you choose to be, you can be part of a very different community and culture and this can be revitalising.

In addition to adventure, many teachers are drawn to international teaching as they feel 'driven away' by the current systems of scrutiny in the UK, which include Ofsted. One teacher explained:

> *"I taught in the UK for 5 years. I initially loved it but the pressures of teaching in the UK were slowly extinguishing my spark for teaching and I was ready to quit the profession altogether."*

Teaching abroad offers both excitement and conversely, challenge. Moving to a new country often begins with a 'honeymoon' period, where everything is interestingly different. You may see only positives around you, comparing all you experience favourably to your last residence. Then, after this period, you may begin to see these differences as problems. This period of adjustment is called 'culture shock'. All your reasons for the move may pale into insignificance if you become irritated and unhappy within your new environment.

I speak of how to combat culture shock in Chapter 6, but at this stage, it is helpful to be reflective of how you are as a person and whether teaching abroad would be a good 'fit' for you and your dependents. Ask yourself:

> Do you enjoy travel and adventure?
> Are you open to new experiences?
> Are you patient enough to deal with visa issues and, quite often, bureaucracy?
> Are you adaptable to variants of the National Curriculum for England or other curricula?
> Can you cope with differing or limited resources or classroom space/facilities?
> Are you happy to work within a school with teachers from other countries, as well as parents and children who may be very different to what you are used to?
> Are you able to accept that you may encounter difficulties where you may not have support, both within and outside of school?
> Do you make friends easily?
> Can you be away from family and friends for an extended period should you need to?
> Are you willing to 'start again' in a new home, new country, and new school?

Can I teach abroad?

This guide presumes that you are already a fully qualified teacher holding a teaching qualification or licence that allows you to teach in international schools. These qualifications may be gained worldwide; however, they need to be accredited by a 'western' institution or university. There are positions for unqualified teachers within international schools but these are less common and to find them you may need to use an agency (discussed further on pages 21-26).

Whilst this book will benefit all budding international school teachers, the advice is most relevant to teachers holding a British teaching qualification with QTS, seeking their first international post in an English-medium international school. Most teachers in this position are English speakers. However, if English is not your first language, there are a range of schools around the world in which teachers from all nationalities can work.

Native English speakers

The majority of international schools look for qualified, native speakers of the language of instruction of the school; for example, a British curriculum school may look for teachers from the UK. However, teachers from other native English speaking countries are often employed in British schools, especially if they have training or experience of teaching the National Curriculum for England. Residents from countries considered native English speaking include the UK, Australia, New Zealand, Canada, South Africa, and the United States. American, Canadian and Australian international schools often favour teachers from their own respective countries. This is likely less to do with accent but more reflective of the knowledge required to teach their curriculum. Further, International Baccalaureate (IB) schools are not affiliated to any particular nationality but seek teachers who have experience and training within their curriculum. A general rule may be applied whereby schools will often (but not exclusively) search for experience of the taught curriculum. Some schools are more flexible and this could be because they have a more open outlook on pedagogy, high staff turnover, or are considered 'hardship' postings.

Non-native English speakers

If you are a native European, there are also international schools where instruction is in a European language, for example French schools, German schools, etc. Within the EU and in several worldwide locations, there are schools that offer a bilingual program with both a European language and English taught in conjunction with one another. Therefore, there are also opportunities for native

English speakers to work within these schools. If you teach a specific language, you may also be accepted into any international school where that language is taught at Primary or Secondary level. Finally, there are also European (Union) schools throughout the EU whose mission is to teach dependents of EU-institution employees in their own language. These schools employ teachers whose native language can be any EU language, but they must also be bilingual in another EU language.

This doesn't mean that you cannot get a job in an international school if you are not a native speaker in the language of instruction, but these opportunities are more difficult to find, often due to government restrictions for working visas. It is worth approaching recruitment companies and schools that are currently advertising roles directly to find out if they will employ you. One international teacher explained:

> *"Local schools (private and public) in my host country ask for candidates from native speaking countries and do not hire anyone who doesn't hold a passport from the six "native English speaking countries" recognised by the government; International schools are more flexible but the paperwork required is enormous, again more so due to government policies rather than the schools themselves."*

When should I move abroad?

If you fulfil the relevant language requirements, the next consideration is at what point in your career you should think about moving abroad to teach. If you have a preferred country or region in mind, it makes sense to investigate the school requirements thoroughly. For example, many international schools look for two or even three years' teaching experience. Recent experience within your own home country is quite an advantage, as you can provide insight and offer training to your colleagues in new developments.

Many British teachers choose to complete their Newly Qualified Teacher (NQT) induction period (one year) plus a further year as a teacher within the UK. Such experience can be useful before moving abroad, as it provides a benchmark as to what the UK expectations are within a standard British state school.

Methods for securing a teaching role abroad

Prior to a job search, you should begin to build up your CV. Support your current school in projects which highlight how you are a good team-player within the school and wider community; furthermore, include initiatives which set you apart from other teachers. Investing in English as an Additional Language (EAL) courses and observing colleagues who teach non-native children would also support your application.

Once you begin a job search, collate all the information you need to create a 'bare bones' CV. Such information should include:

1. Personal information such as full name, email, LinkedIn profile address, address (current city and country only) and contact number/Skype contact. It is a matter of preference whether or not you wish to include a professional photo (headshot). For inclusivity it is not necessary to attach a photo, unless an employer requests it.
2. Your work and education history, courses attended specific to teaching, voluntary work, and interests. If you have worked with EAL children, this should also feature within your CV.

Later, you will need to develop your CV and letter of intent/philosophy to reflect the requirements of each individual school.

International schools are beginning to post their positions earlier and earlier, therefore it is recommended you begin your search around September for an August start. This is approximately one year before you would start the job. This is not true for all countries; Singapore, Australia, New Zealand, and South America, for example, have earlier start dates. Many southern hemisphere schools begin the new academic year in March and some begin their school year in January. So be aware of the academic start dates and adjust your search accordingly.

Most teachers use one or several of the following methods to find international teaching positions:

Internet job sites

The Times Education Supplement (TES) website is where I have found my teaching jobs. Throughout the year, I also have a look to identify schools I may like to work for in the future, as the schools' ethos and their priorities are often clearly stated in their recruitment ads.

Websites such as 'Guardian Education' and TES are excellent starting points. The jobs advertised are regarded by teachers as 'legitimate', and are mostly posted by schools themselves. Teachers can search for positions using different criteria, including the preferred country, key stage, type of contract, and school.

Furthermore, these sites allow you to set up notifications whereby you will be informed of suitable jobs via email. Applying for jobs in this way allows you to know exactly what you are applying for, as they are usually posted directly by the school. Schools will usually request a cover letter. If the contents of the cover letter are not stated, follow the guidelines in Chapter 2. A cover letter generally requires you to describe your interest in the school and details which expressly relate to the criteria required for the specific job. In addition, a CV or online application may also be required.

Many teachers recommend using internet job sites. However, others felt that this method did not lead to as many interviews or expressions of interest when compared to using a recruitment agency. For example, one teacher explained that she had applied to over 70 schools without interest. You should be aware that it may take *many* tailored applications to find a job using this method. Yet, one colleague maintained:

> *"TES is the easiest system I have ever used to find a job. I applied for three schools and received three interviews. I like how you can specify the exact role you want and the country."*

Applying directly to an educational group

This is relevant when a school is part of a larger organisation, such as Nord Anglia, Dulwich, Harrow, GEMS, Quality Schools International (QSI) and Shell Schools, to name a few. These companies have schools worldwide, or at least several within a region. Often these organisations have their own hiring procedures, in addition to applying directly to the school. Therefore, it is best to check their websites to find out how they hire teachers if you have identified a school run by one of these companies.

Applying to a programme

Another option is to apply for a programme to teach overseas. Often these are for roles teaching English as a foreign or additional language (EFL/EAL). However, if you are unsure of working within an international school and would like to try working within local schools, then this could be a great option. Countries and recruiters include Brunei (CfBT), Japan (JET Program), and the United Arab Emirates (Government Schools).

> My first experience working abroad was with a program in Japan. This was as an English teacher within various local schools. I feel this first experience supported my move into international teaching, as I had a range of experiences with many different EAL children across age ranges.

Recruitment agencies

Generally speaking, agencies have staff who will, once you have created your profile, interview you or email you to support you in finding a school. Many offer their own job listings. These companies may be free for teachers to use, or you may have to pay a one-off fee or annual subscription. If they are free, they will take a commission for placing you from the school. Several teachers believed that some schools provide a slightly adjusted salary to take into account the agent's fee. Teachers were also concerned that some free agencies may receive a higher commission from certain schools, therefore this may influence their selections for you. However, this is certainly not the case for all agencies, as some are very ethical companies. This is something you could research and ask the agency you choose to use about.

Several teachers agreed that free agencies are excellent for teachers new to international teaching, as often the paid agencies work with more established schools who want experienced international teachers. The contrary argument here, though, is that paid agencies work with more established schools, if this is what you are looking for.

An established school should be well-accredited by a globally recognised accrediting body and therefore is very likely to be an academically-sound place to work. The Accreditation Service for International Schools, Colleges and Universities (ASIC) explain that accreditation is important, as it raises the profile of the school. It assures the public, students, parents, and other stakeholders as to the quality of a school and its commitment to high standards through a system of continuous improvement.

Other teachers feel that using an agency does give you a better chance at being placed in a reputable school, rather than a school which has simply placed an advert on a job search page. The reason for this is that agencies often visit schools and therefore they connect with the management team and gain an understanding of how the school operates. Further, some agencies visit schools in order to ensure that teachers and schools are a good 'fit'.

'Free for teachers' agencies

As these agencies are paid for placing a teacher within a school, they do not take any registration fee from the teacher. Below I discuss several recommended companies, all of which are online, therefore can be accessed easily using a search engine.

Teachanywhere

To apply for roles, the applicant can create their CV with the support of agency staff, or simply submit a CV they have created. Following this, a consultant will contact you and ask about your aspirations for international teaching, in terms of your situation, academics, types of schools that would be suitable, and what you are looking for. Then, they will complete a profile and contact your referees. The consultant will advise you of positions available. If any roles appeal to you, the consultant will then send a job description. Teachanywhere states that they will use their knowledge of both schools and applicants to ensure that candidates are well matched to the school. As the consultant takes care of the application process, there should be no need to write a cover letter. Should you be shortlisted, a video call interview will take place, followed by a job offer if successful. Teachers report that they are happy with the service and they feel the company is trustworthy.

Teacher Horizons

This agency states on its website that they have the best teaching positions in the world, with a community discussion board to support teachers even further. Their specialist advisors are teachers themselves and they offer feedback on both a candidate's profile and CV. They work with schools to recommend their candidates directly to the school principal. They state that an applicant's CV is therefore fast tracked in the recruitment process. Teacher Horizons advisors visit the schools they work with and speak to the teachers as well as the leadership team to find out about the types of international teachers they are looking for. They also claim that they check the international schools are good places to work, thereby getting a sense of the lifestyle that international teachers lead based on the package they offer. They do not offer teacher recruitment fairs but they are able to give key information about salary and benefits for international jobs. Teachers describe this agency as offering a personalised service, cultivating trust and genuinely caring about the teachers and the schools they work with.

Teach Away

This agency places teachers in EFL positions, international schools, government programmes, universities, and language institutions. Teachers register on the website, fill out a teacher profile, and then search for positions. As a profile is created on the system, teachers can apply directly through the site. The agency also offers training programmes for Teaching English as a Foreign Language (TEFL). Teachers are generally happy with this company, as they set up interviews in countries where teachers want to go.

TIC Recruitment

Like others, this agency offers to guide teachers through the process of application. They present an applicant's CV to the management team for a role the applicant chooses from their database. They ensure that they 'vet' every school that they have on their books, but they encourage their candidates to research fully the school's methods, values, salary and benefits, and the local area. As a smaller company, they claim to offer a more personalised experience and they have been specialising in this field for 14 years. During this time, they have worked with hundreds of international schools in over 80 countries. They work with mainly British-style schools, defined by the curriculum they teach and the mainly British staff. Many of these schools use a combination of International Primary Curriculum (IPC), the National Curriculum for England, and IB programmes. Teachers are generally happy with the experience and reported that both Teach Away and TIC had contacted them later to check that their contract had been honoured after they had been appointed.

Edvectus

This agency is often recommended by teachers as they feel supported with each step of their application and especially in having their preferences heard. Edvectus claims to be an innovative company that combines recruitment with a learning portal for teachers who wish to improve their teaching skills and enhance their knowledge of international curricula and working abroad. They aim to minimise a client's risk by hiring teachers who are qualified, screened, trained, and informed about the school, region, and challenges beforehand. The recruitment consultants are ex-teachers with international experience.

Paid agencies

Teachers argue that the schools presented by free agencies are likely more limited in scope than the big, paid for, agencies in international recruitment, such as ISS/Schrole Advantage, and Search Associates.

Paid agencies require a registration fee from teachers to enrol for their service and database. The schools also pay a fee to these companies. Similar to the 'free' agencies, these agencies create a profile with the applicant. However, the profile can be viewed directly by schools. The agencies provide a personal advisor and a database of jobs that often offer a level of detail you wouldn't get from applying directly to a school, such as salary expectations and the demographics of both teachers and students. They also operate job fairs, which you can attend with the hope of securing a job (for a full discussion on job fairs, see page 61). However, the emphasis is for the applicant to seek roles using the database.

There is an on-going debate on international teaching forums as to whether a paid agency is really worth the money. Some teachers complain that the positions they are offered are often in locations they did not want and then, when suitable positions were available, they had to 'do all the work' themselves. This was echoed by others who felt they still did all the searching on the database and applied for each job individually, which is time-consuming. Conversely, other teachers have said that they have had wonderful support from their advisors and have found excellent roles. Many feel that the more popular schools only recruit using the paid agencies.

Search Associates

As a paid agency, teachers currently pay a membership fee which lasts for three years or until a job is secured. Search Associates have a huge network of, in 2021, 730 member schools in over 120 countries. They offer a large database which allows for comparisons between schools, as well as offering details about expat packages, not just salaries. Teachers believe that the agency carefully 'vets' schools and matches teachers well and will remove schools from their database that do not treat teachers well. Furthermore, candidates explained that an advantage of Search Associates is their experienced, proactive team. The associates are available for support until a candidate finds a job. Yet, some teachers feel that not all associates are as good as others; and that they do not always represent the 'best' schools. A further complaint was that the signing up process to the agency takes a lot of time and energy.

ISS/Schrole Advantage

ISS/Schrole Advantage has schools across the globe; in Africa, Central America, Central Asia, East Asia, North America, South America, South Asia, South East Asia, the Middle East, and Europe. In 2020, they were working with approximately 400 schools. Teachers pay an annual membership fee. Some teachers feel that this agency offers a better match to schools over other agencies. Teachers also find their school database excellent and have commented that ISS/Schrole Advantage requires comparatively lower fees compared to Search Associates.

Recruitment databases

A further option is to subscribe to a paid 'jobs database', one of which is joyjobs.com. The company was started to assist new international teachers without connections or prior international experience, but with 'a desire to change their lives'. They do support teachers to make a 'recruiting profile' which evidences your professional and personal credibility. The site has been established for more than twenty years and teachers have named this database as being useful in their search.

Approaching schools directly

Another option to secure a teaching role is to approach schools directly, prior to a role being advertised. This is especially useful if you have narrowed down your options to one or several countries in which you wish to work. Complete your own internet research using search terms such as 'International schools in (insert country)'. You may need to further narrow down your search to certain cities in order to find international schools. Then, check each school's website and contact their Human Resources department directly.

Send a prospective email with your CV. Make sure you keep your cover letter brief and to the point, mentioning why the school has caught your interest and what you can offer to develop the school (for further discussion on cover letters, see page 56). Once you have narrowed down your school choices, regularly check their websites to look for any suitable job postings. If a position does become available, you may wish to arrange a visit (see page 62). Contacting schools directly can sometimes be a good way to 'get ahead of the game', before the usual hiring period.

> I researched schools in Thailand and I had some excellent candid replies from several Heads, which made me even more interested in the schools! But do not be put off if you do not receive a reply, as some schools do not respond to unsolicited emails.

Social media: Facebook

Do not underestimate social media! International school jobs are often posted on Facebook job boards. In Appendix B, I have made a list of teaching job boards to support your search and international teachers/expat boards. Once a member of these boards, you can inquire if teachers know of a job available in their school or ask for recommendations of schools in the country you wish to work. Teachers may also post listings from their school on these sites. Therefore, this provides the opportunity to directly message the teacher to find out more about each listing. Using these pages can connect you with present or former teachers at the school. Networking in this way is key to building up your knowledge of the school. One colleague explained:

> *"There is no one you can get a more honest opinion about a place from than the staff who actually work*

there. Many school websites look really flashy and glamourous but the reality of working at those schools is not great at all."

Social media: LinkedIn and Twitter

It is important that you update your LinkedIn profile and state that you are looking for work. Make sure you list keywords in your profile which describe you, your ethos, and reflect the school you wish to work in. Ensure that you have any courses and voluntary work related to your role listed on your profile. Connect with recruiters and the schools you are interested in on both LinkedIn and Twitter. Further, connect with colleagues and professionals within teaching, and groups that work within the age range you teach. Regularly review the information and post any blogs or articles you have read that you feel are worthy of sharing. A recruiter may look at how active you are in your field. Many schools have LinkedIn profiles where they advertise work, so check this regularly for job openings. You can also set the roles you are looking for on LinkedIn, so you will be emailed jobs directly. If a school is technologically active, their Twitter feed will give you great insight into the school and an opportunity to 'like' and comment on their posts, making your name known to a prospective employer. Further, following teachers at the school and key professionals in your field will give you the opportunity to network with them and make you aware of the current trends within the school that you can discuss at an interview.

Personal recommendations from teachers

Ask around your teacher friends and colleagues, to discover which schools/countries teachers recommend working in. They may have contacts still in those schools which you could ask for. Sometimes having this 'way in' can support your application, or at least direct you to the 'right' person to impress within a school. Again, if they are willing, such contacts are an excellent source of knowledge about the school.

Contact previous employers and colleagues

If this is not your first move abroad, you may wish to consider contacting previous Headteachers or Deputy Heads of schools, to see if they have any current positions within their new school. If you enjoyed working with them previously this can be quite a reassuring aspect of considering their new school. Similarly, keep in contact with colleagues when they 'move on' from your school. They will be able to compare their current school with the school you work in, which will offer invaluable insights.

Overall, international teachers believe that there is not a one-stop-shop anymore in finding a teaching position abroad. The best method to conduct a job search is to use several methods: join agencies and also complete your own search. Ask around and check forums for advice and leads.

Choosing where in the world to work

Once you start your job search, you will become aware of the location(s) available to you. It is likely you will feel drawn to certain countries due to previous knowledge or experience, whether that be from a holiday or a personal recommendation. You may already be very clear about where in the world you would like to live. However, there are some important considerations, which are detailed below.

The physical environment

Consider what type of environment would suit you and your family best. If you love the outdoors, mountains, and greenery, then not all countries would be suitable for you. This lifestyle can be found, however, in parts of China, Taiwan, Europe, and South/

Central America, for example. Should you want access to great 'western' style shopping, then consider developed countries such as Singapore, Hong Kong, larger cities in China, and the UAE. If you are looking for beaches rather than city life, look out for roles in Thailand, Vietnam, Philippines and the Caribbean. Teaching roles in holiday destinations really do exist! A tip would be to use Google Maps to look closely at the school and the surrounding areas. You can pan into street view and virtually 'walk' around the area.

AQI, natural disasters, and political unrest

This is a significant area to investigate. Air quality, particularly within Asia, is becoming more of a concern. A quick check of the air quality in a particular city can be found on *IQAir AirVisual* (either on the website or app). This will let you view the current AQI levels and compare levels for cities around the world.

Further, natural disasters, for example earthquakes, occur frequently in countries located on geological fault lines, such as Taiwan, Japan, the Philippines, and parts of Central and South America. These, alongside typhoons and tropical storms, can devastate countries with poor infrastructures, such as the Philippines. This may affect your school as well as your home. It is wise to reflect upon your ideal climate. You may consider it preferable to live in a tropical climate, without seasons, yet some teachers can struggle with humidity, extreme cold, or a lack of seasons. Therefore, check the year-round temperatures of the countries which interest you, as well as their weather conditions.

In addition, countries within certain continents, such as Africa and South America, can be susceptible to both civil and political unrest. Similarly, political tensions exist in some Asian countries, including between North Korea and South Korea, and between China and Hong Kong and Taiwan. These are just a few examples and, as situations constantly change, I will avoid providing a list, but instead encourage you to seek up to date information on your country or region of interest.

Whichever country you decide to move to, it is important to have contacts in the host country and resources at home on which you can rely. Any country can experience civil or political unrest; even a seemingly stable country. Depending on your school, you may not be the priority in the event of difficult times, so it is important to consider this carefully. One teacher remarked:

> *"In two schools, [in] the first [where] I experienced a revolution and [in] the second the COVID 19 pandemic, the bottom line was not a focus on staff wellbeing."*

Country/visa requirements for international teachers

As you search for a role, it is important to bear in mind that to acquire a working visa in some countries is more difficult than others. In some instances, there can be age, qualifications, and/or passport restrictions for working visa applications. Therefore, if you are over 50, it is worth researching the visa age limits for the country. *Joy Jobs.com* provides a general list of these.

Some countries and/or employers require more advanced qualifications than others, although it is possible to work in some international schools with just a Bachelor's degree. For example, in Dubai's top schools in 2021, a minimum requirement is a Master's degree in a relevant specialism, a teaching certification, and three years' experience (Lansing). The UAE Ministry of Education requires that all teachers have a 'teaching certification', which can include TEFL, TESOL, or CELTA, however this is only useful if you wish to teach English only. Furthermore, in some countries (including the UK) the PGCE allows you teach within any age range within a school, as long as you have QTS. However, other countries, such as New Zealand, have more stringent requirements for Early Childhood teachers. To teach this age range in New

Zealand, teachers must have a specific Early Childhood degree or Graduate Diploma of Teaching within Early Childhood (careers. govt.nz).

A final restriction is your passport. If you do not hold a passport from a known 'native' English speaking country, you could encounter difficulty due to school or visa restrictions. This may apply even if you have a full and relevant teaching qualification. A colleague explained:

> *"In my first year in Kuwait, I taught at a British School which has a terrible reputation. I was aware of that from the research I had done, but it was my only way into the country, as with a Cypriot Passport (not a British or an American one), it was very hard to get a job anywhere in the Middle East and, as I was desperate for a post there at that point, I just took on the job. It is much easier for anyone with a passport from an English-speaking country to get a job in this region."*

Expectations

Reflect upon your reasons for wishing to relocate and consider if these outweigh your reasons for staying at home. You will very likely experience a level of difficulty, disappointment, or culture shock at some point during your transition. It is important that you focus on the possible professional, personal, and lifestyle improvements. When researching a country and school, make a list of both the positive and negative aspects that you are likely to encounter.

Ensure that you have realistic expectations by discussing the school and country with people working at the school and expats in the wider community (for discussions on how to connect with others see pages 27 and 53). It is particularly important that you research the staff demographic of the school. You can usually find staff profiles on the website, which would give an indication of the age/gender demographic of the teachers. If not, this is an acceptable question to ask at interview or to the school's HR team. One young, single teacher explained:

> *"[I settled well due to] the fact that everyone was so welcoming. I liked that there were lots of other young people who had also moved there on their own so were up for exploring and doing things together."*

Nevertheless, there are some factors which you cannot control. You may have visited a country on holiday and be keen to move there. Yet, a permanent move to a country may present a quite different reality to your holiday. Take your first move and subsequent moves as a new adventure. If possible, relocate somewhere very different to the UK or your last placement, so that comparisons are more difficult to make. Should you really regret the move, consider a return. There is no harm in going back, as several of my colleagues have.

Healthcare

Research the quality of healthcare available in the location you are considering. Are there international hospitals or English-speaking doctors/clinics? How developed is the healthcare system? In some countries there is a 'visiting' dentist who is not available all the time, or, for serious issues, you would need to be airlifted to a hospital. If you have any long-term health complaints or conditions, these should be discussed with the school. It is important to ascertain if the country has the infrastructure to support your needs. This is explored in greater depth in Chapter 6.

Transport links

Investigate the surroundings in terms of transport. Is it an easy place to get from A to B by public transport? What is the traffic like? If you like to drive, it may be extremely expensive to buy a car, with high levels of tax on purchases (such as Vietnam).

In many countries the norm is to buy a motorbike or bicycle to get around. Consider if this is something you would be willing to do. In some places, taxis and Ubers are incredibly cheap. Again, if you like to travel around, research the price of transportation such as taxis, buses, and trains. In cities such as Jakarta, traffic is a huge problem so a short journey can take hours. Consider how this may impact on your journey to school and ability to travel.

Further, contemplate the availability of wider travel from your location of choice. Research the distance from the airport you will use and the transport links it provides. Before deciding on a location, check the travel time to/from your home and favourite holiday destinations, if this is important to you. Further, if the location is remote, you may find that flights are infrequent, which could really impact upon travel. Access to transport is further explored in Chapter 5.

Culture of the country and school

When researching the country/countries which interest you, decide whether it is a culture in which you could work and live. Ask yourself what you may need to change to live within a certain society? This is a really important question.

For example, in many Arab countries, religious beliefs are central to the society and may limit or ban pursuits you enjoy, such as drinking alcohol. As an expat you would need to follow these rules and expectations. In communist societies, such as China, practices which may feel very normal, such as accessing Facebook and the BBC, need to be done via a VPN. News can be censored, as well as the curricula taught, and there is a curtailment of free expression (Amnesty International 14).

Some countries have restrictions on females for example. Other countries can have a preference for lighter skinned foreigners, and treat individuals with darker skins differently. In a country with a strong religious following, such as Egypt, females need to cover their shoulders and knees in 30-plus degree weather. Furthermore, the 'call to prayer' can also be something you need to get used to, beginning early in the morning. One teacher who had been based in Egypt explained:

> "...no matter how much I was covered up, I experienced looks and comments by males and females, whilst I watched men walking around in shorts and vest tops. Personally, this, along with other negative experiences (due to my being female), made me very unhappy to continue [living there] beyond a two-year contract."

You may feel a certain 'fit' within a culture. Many factors influence this; the ability to express yourself, the temperament of the people, or the abundant pursuits which you enjoy. The landscape can be a huge deciding factor.

Local cuisine, and the availability of other cuisines, deserves a mention here, too. In some countries, there can be a lack of international food options. For some international teachers, this is a significant consideration. For example, countries such as Taiwan may have what many consider to be excellent local cuisine. However, within the residential areas of Taipei, close to the two main international schools, international restaurants are not so common and, where they are available, they are expensive.

Yet, if you miss home comforts, there are international companies that will ship your favourite foods to you. Similarly, in some countries you can receive shipping from companies such as Amazon and online retailers. You can check whether these companies would ship to your chosen area (for a list of shippers of 'western' foods/products see Appendix B).

Another area to investigate is just how open-minded and accepting your country of interest is to single-sex relationships, other cultures, and skin colour. Some countries have a hidden hierarchy in terms of the most and least respected expats or immigrants.

My relocation to Vietnam felt like a 'breath of fresh air' in comparison to Egypt. Due to the more liberal environment, I feel that I personally 'fit' better in Asia. My move to Taiwan was also successful. Taiwan has a very accepting culture. In addition, the abundant opportunities for beaches and hiking all made a great fit for me.

However, it is not only the culture of the country you need to investigate. As you research the school, you may wish to keep in mind their inclusion and diversity programmes for students, as well as how they represent the global community they serve. One colleague elaborated on this very succinctly:

> *"The school has the most diverse student body in the country but this is not mirrored in the staff body where in my 10 years I have seen two South Asian teachers (including me), two teachers from South East Asian countries and four teachers representing the black community."*

Language

Investigate the main spoken language of the country and, should English not be widely spoken, reflect upon whether you would be willing to learn. Around the world, English is often spoken in major cities, but outside of these areas you may need to master the basics of the local language. If you do struggle to learn languages, think about how this may affect you in your day-to-day communications with shopkeepers or taxi drivers.

Moving abroad as a couple or with children

I discuss both opportunities and difficulties for trailing spouses and moving with children in greater detail in Chapter 6. However, at this stage it is important to consider as a couple or as a family whether you would be happy together abroad. Would all members be able to cope with the transition? Ensure you have these conversations now and if one partner is more reluctant, it is better to voice all concerns before a move. You all need to be on the same page and willing to embark on a complete change. This will involve all of you leaving family, friends, and a community you may have known for a long time.

Different types of international school

Be aware that there is no clear definition of what constitutes an 'international school'. A school does not need to meet any criteria to be labelled 'international' (MacDonald 193). Although there are some similarities, overall international schools differ greatly to state systems.

International schools may be single-sex or coeducational; include a large age range, from pre-nursery to high school, or specialize in a much smaller age range, such as middle or high school, the numbers of pupils may vary to from 20 to in excess of 3000 students, they may follow a particular denomination or educational philosophy, such as play-based, student-led inquiry, or highly eco-centric, such as the Green School in Bali. Many of these establishments can be difficult to define, however the most common types of international school are outlined below.

The 'international-ness' of the students within an international school

Hill describes the 'pure' type of international school as having a very culturally diverse population, ideally without one nationality over represented (8). These schools are often private and independent, teaching an international education program. Many were originally created to service internationally-mobile parents. Hill states that some schools use the label of 'international' but cater predominantly for students from a particular nation and receive corresponding government subsidies (9), exemplified by the 'European schools' discussed previously. They may offer one or more national curricula.

In contrast to the 'pure' type of international school, other international schools may serve a culturally homogenous local population, who can afford-and want to pay for-a western education. These schools may include the word 'international' in their title because it sounds prestigious, or because it legitimately reflects the international mindedness of the educational program of the school (Hill 9). The owners may be 'foreign' themselves, but there may or may not be a prerequisite that students hold an international passport. Some of these schools may operate a quota system regarding the number of international students (with an international passport) versus local students. One Headteacher explained:

> *"Schools can often determine their quota. In some countries, marketing can also play a role, as local parents can prefer the idea that there is also a quota of non-local children."*

When considering these different types of school, whether predominantly expat student or local population schools, you may wish to consider whether your desire to teach internationally comes from a desire to teach a diverse range of students or perhaps your interests lie in supporting the local population become global citizens. If you have children who will attend the school this will be an important consideration. Often schools which cater to the local population will have local children who will prefer to speak their native language outside of taught lessons. In addition, a school which caters to the local population may focus on developing and using the local language in lessons and around the school, through timetabled language lessons or using a bilingual method (bilingual schools are discussed further below). Conversely, a school with a significant expat community is far more likely to use English as a common language to communicate at all times in the school day.

For-profit or not-for-profit international schools

International schools are either for-profit or not-for-profit. For-profit schools will usually be overseen by a director/owner, who has a vested interest in providing education whilst making as much profit as possible. An article by William Scarborough explains that these schools are subject to taxes like other businesses and the owner makes all major decisions, although staff and parents may be approached for their opinion on decisions pertaining to the school. Many for-profit schools are run by large companies, such as Cognita and GEMS Education. Scarborough maintains that these schools are essentially businesses. Therefore, as a business, allocations of resources are considered in terms of the overall profit margin of the school. They are likely to have shareholders and investors. There may be more of an emphasis on financial success than the wellbeing of teachers and the ability to retain them. Reflecting on her experience within a for-profit school, a colleague stressed that a new international teacher should be aware:

> *"…that the needs of the children and what would be best educationally aren't as important necessarily as in a state system. Owners can wield a great deal of power, as can parents, because they are fee-paying and want value for money. Further, choices on how to furnish/resource a school are made by business people, not educators. Management can be stuck between staff with an education focus and owners with a monetary focus, which can lead to compromised outcomes."*

This does not mean that a for-profit school will lack all necessary resources, as they will need to compete with other international schools in the local area. The facilities are likely to be 'showier', as this is what often impresses their clients: the parents of prospective pupils. However, this is not always the case, should there be a shortage of school places for the community a school serves.

In comparison, Scarborough discussed how not-for-profit schools have the aim of reinvesting any profits back into the school, and exist to satisfy a mission and not to make a profit for an individual or company. They are not likely to have shareholders, investors, or owners. Instead, they are usually governed by a group of current or former parents or community members who have formed a board of directors or trustees. The directors usually wield extensive power, which includes hiring the headteacher, setting the educational vision, and directing the school's financial strategies.

Generally speaking, not-for-profit schools are well-resourced, especially in terms of teaching materials and day-to-day resources. There may also be a budget for resources. Further, as profits are re-invested, there may well be funds available for personal development.

With all of this in mind, I again emphasise that thorough research of your prospective school is a stronger indicator of staff wellbeing, academic standards, and resourcing than simply considering whether it is a for-profit or not-for-profit school. Exemplifying this, a teacher discusses the difference between two for-profit schools, both run by the same company:

> *"I initially worked in a for-profit British international school which was run more as a business than an educational institution...but the school was quite well resourced and there was professional development training offered for staff. From there, I moved to a school which was much smaller and had a real family feel to it. Although it was run by the same company, it was more like an educational institution rather than a business. I certainly felt very valued as a staff member there."*

Scarborough also discusses some differences between for-profit and not-for-profit schools which are worth considering:

Personal connection: A not-for-profit school is administered by unpaid board members, often parents, who have experience with-and likely an emotional connection to-the school. A for-profit school run by a CEO or company may not have any connection to the actual educational experiences of the students, nor a personal connection to the school.

Models of governance: Within a not-for-profit school, the major decisions are made after discussions involving a group, which will at least include the board; whilst a for-profit school's decisions may not take into account parent and student opinions.

Relationships with parents: As a not-for-profit school's board has a connection to the school community, it will need to listen to aggrieved parents if a decision is not popular. However, the CEO or owners of a for-profit school may not feel the need to listen to complaints and prefer to let parents go elsewhere.

Focus on education: Whilst a for-profit school might argue it will be more efficient and satisfy demand better than competitors, a not-for-profit school can argue that, as it does not allocate any of its budget to investors or shareholders, it can do more with its proceeds and focus on education rather than a profit motive. One colleague, a director of his own for-profit school, explained:

> *"I feel relationships with parents strongly depend on the size of the school, as for-profit schools will often 'give in' to parents so that the school 'keeps' the children and therefore the profit."*

Having worked in both profit and not-for-profit schools, I feel that the latter was far better equipped in terms of classroom resources and ICT. The for-profit school had outstanding facilities, yet I had minimal resources to teach with and ended up buying and creating a lot of my own. I didn't have access to any kind of resourcing 'budget' within the two for-profit schools in which I have worked, but in the not-for-profit school I have ordered classroom resources.

School fees, hiring, and salary

Although this is discussed in greater depth later, it is worth mentioning here that school fees can vary greatly, even within one city or region. The difference in fees may be due to enhanced facilities, or it may translate to better salaries for staff and therefore the school is able to attract the 'best' candidates.

Often schools do not release a pay scale as they would be required to do in the UK. Some job advertisements will state 'salary matches UK main pay scale' so you can deduce your salary. Other advertisements state 'substantial remuneration' or similar. Some schools will not provide their salary offer until after interview and may not provide a salary scale even when you are employed there.

It is not necessarily the 'best' schools that offer their scale freely, however it is something to have in mind when you consider how ethical a school is in terms of paying staff. Staff may be employed on different salaries and contract benefits within the same school. Schools eager to gain or maintain accreditation are likely to be transparent about their salary scales, as many accreditation bodies will mark a school down if the scales are not published.

Finally, the type of staff the school hires is worth looking into. Should the school advertise a hiring policy of recruiting unqualified teachers, this is likely an indication of the standards of teaching and learning within the school. In certain areas of the school, such as Early Years, where local staff or non-western trained staff are often hired to the greatest extent, this may also limit your choices if, for example, you are an Early Years specialist.

Location

Where your school is located, in addition to the demand for international schooling in that area, may well affect its quality and standards. If there is less competition for excellence with other international schools, the school is more likely to retain its pupils due to the lack of choice in the area. Schools in cities where there is a great deal of choice need to maintain their reputation and academic standing within the community in order to maintain enrolment.

Reputation and academic standing

International schools can be further categorised in terms of their reputation and academic attainment levels. Please be aware these are *generalisations* taken from my colleagues and my own personal experience.

Well-established international schools (often called 'top tier' or 'Tier 1' international schools)

These schools have usually been in operation for a substantial time period. They have a good reputation internationally with all stakeholders (parents, teachers, students, and recruiters). They are likely known for excellent facilities and are well-resourced. Such schools are usually inspected and then approved by international accreditation bodies such as the Council of International Schools (CIS), Council of British International Schools (COBIS), or ASIC. These schools will generally follow established western curricula, such as the National Curriculum for England or IB.

Their international teacher packages can be substantial in terms of their salary and benefits; therefore, their hiring policies are likely to be very stringent. When recruiting, management are likely to select more experienced teachers rather than first-time international teachers. Often the 'onboarding' experience and induction for new teachers is very well-organised and helpful.

As they are well-accredited, they are very likely to have sound educational ethics. However, this does not mean that staff morale will be high, and they can be workplaces where teachers struggle to achieve a work-life balance. Often teachers mention that although these schools treat their staff well, their expectations of staff are very demanding in terms of workload and extra-curricular responsibilities. If these schools are part of a wider educational company, they may feel quite corporate or restrictive due to policies and directives from that company.

Aspiring top tier schools ('Tier 2' schools)

They may have some similar credentials to the 'Tier 1' schools, but they are likely not as established, lack the facilities, and/or are less reputable than Tier 1 schools. These schools are often striving towards an accreditation or further accreditation(s), therefore, when working within these schools, achieving this is likely to take precedence.

To attain accreditation, teachers often need to work in accreditation committees, to help collate the relevant documentation required. As this becomes a main driver for the school, ensuring the wellbeing of staff can become less of a priority. As an inspection date approaches, all priorities will shift towards that. Such schools can feel as though they have something to prove and therefore a teacher may feel a significant proportion of their work is just to 'tick boxes' and complete paperwork to satisfy the priorities set by the Senior Leadership Team. This is of course not always the case, as one colleague explained:

"My school in Brunei was a Tier 2 and moved into Tier 1 whilst I was there. The positives were that I was part of the process of creating policies and procedures, as we moved towards our first CIS accreditation. This was really empowering and enabling for us as a staff, as we had a voice."

If you are considering a school which is striving towards becoming a Tier 1 school, plan the interview questions you might ask carefully and reflect upon the questions the school asks of you. Attempt to ascertain the wellbeing of the staff by contacting current teachers and questioning them on what they feel are the school's priorities, what the workload expectations are, and what the current morale within the school is like.

I have worked in aspiring top tier schools. I would argue they are difficult places to work. In general, I felt excessive paperwork and unnecessary meetings were the norm, whilst teaching and learning fell by the wayside. New initiatives were frequently introduced to 'improve' the school, with little training, time to consolidate, or care for staff wellbeing.

Mid-level international schools

These schools may be newly established, or have just attained, or be working towards, accreditation. Such schools can be great places to begin your international career. If you are a hard-working teacher, there is often scope for advancement within these schools. Further, as the schools are just beginning to establish themselves, you may be able to contribute to the running and development of the school, adding experience to your CV.

However, it is likely that these schools are only beginning to establish policies and systems. Due to this, there may be an element of disorganisation. They may not offer as much support during the initial induction or onboarding programme, or they may lack professionalism in terms of paying their staff regularly or on time. Therefore, being flexible and adaptable within these schools is key. As the schools are establishing themselves, the salary will likely be lower than the previous two types of school discussed.

In a mid-level international school, I enjoyed autonomy in the workplace as my in-class work was not tightly controlled. As a dedicated teacher, within a year I was offered a leadership role within my department. However, there were problems in terms of resourcing (such as classroom learning resources) and often my salary would be paid late.

International bilingual schools

Whilst other international schools offer the native language of the country as a stand-alone lesson or an extra-curricular activity, these schools usually divide their teaching timetable between English and the language of the country, to varying degrees. Therefore, as a teacher you are likely to work alongside a local teacher, planning and resourcing together. This may be in a 'team-teaching' situation, whereby you teach in the same classroom at the same time, or by sharing a timetable. In this case, you may have two classes that you are responsible for teaching English to, for example, one group in the morning and one in the afternoon.

If you are considering these schools, it is important to ask questions regarding how the school day is run and how the work is divided between yourself and the other teacher. They may follow a curriculum which is not western, such as the Singapore curriculum, or they may use a combination of a recognised western curriculum alongside a curriculum relevant to the host country. Some bilingual schools may not be accredited by international standards. However, this is not the case for all, as some bilingual schools are affiliated with a successful international schools group, such as the CIS-accredited British Vietnamese International School in Vietnam (part of the Nord Anglia group). For example, one secondary teacher working in a bilingual international school felt that both the experience and development professionally really supported their teaching:

> *"[The] language learning focus is an important part of my day to day and has become the norm. Also, I would say that there are parts of the learning relating to language that I would happily take back to the UK."*

A place of work which uses 'International' in its name or claims to be international

This type of school is likely to be small, catering mostly to the local population, with a mix of both national and international staff. The school may follow a curriculum, but it may not be rigid or thorough compared to reputable international schools. The owners can be foreign or may have lived overseas. Often the pay and benefits are significantly lower than the other schools discussed. However, this does not mean the schools are necessarily 'bad' or an environment which would not be good to teach in.

These schools can be excellent places to begin a teaching career and often would not require a teaching qualification. They can attract young, unqualified staff, or older trailing spouses, so it may be less stressful and less pressure to work in these places than in the other types of international schools discussed. However, there is the risk that the school may operate as more of a business than an educational establishment. To discern whether this is the case, it would be a good idea to research both the director and/or the Headteacher to understand the focus of the school. If their vision comes across as the children being at the heart of all they do and their educational practices are clearly valid and evident, then such establishments can offer excellent opportunities for teachers.

Additionally, they may use elements of bilingual teaching and learning similar to bilingual schools. This can often be the case in Early Years and Key Stage 1, when the children are learning both their home language and a second language.

International boarding schools

Boarding schools may offer both a day school and a boarding option, where children can live at the school. They are often very international, as parents can send their children overseas without living in the country themselves. As round-the-clock care is needed for the children, there are usually 'house masters/mistresses' employed who look after the children out of hours. However, working in this type of school often requires extra hours in the evenings and at weekends to look after children who are boarding. A teacher's pay may well reflect this; however, it is important to ask about these 'extra hours' expectations. If you are concerned, ask for your contract to stipulate any such requirements.

International branches of local schools

These schools may already be well-established both structurally and within their community. However, there may be 'push back' from the board and/or community when trying to develop the 'international-ness' of the school. An example of such a school is the 'International School Het Rijnlands Lyceum Oegstgeest.' Their website explains that although the educational programmes of the international school are independent of those at the Dutch school, they are housed within the same building between the aim to create a 'unique meeting place of cultures'. Integration between the Dutch and international department is encouraged whenever possible, be it in the form of theatre productions, sports activities, Model United Nations, or other projects.

'Alternative' curriculum schools

These schools may follow the National Curriculum for England or other approaches such as Waldorf, Montessori, or Reggio. However, how they operate is likely to be very different to a typical British state or independent school. For example, these schools may differ in their pedagogy, focusing on other aspects such as inquiry-led learning, community involvement, or have an eco-focus.

I had the pleasure of visiting an 'alternative' school in Thailand. The school was built around an extensive play area, with open classrooms built into rock. The community was heavily involved in school events, including a weekly community cross-country run based within the school. Although there was technology and a library, both could be affected by damp weather. At the time I visited, I was struck by both how challenging and somewhat liberating a school like this could be.

Company schools

There are some international schools linked to companies, such as Royal Dutch Shell and their affiliate workers. These schools can be in remote areas and cater exclusively for workers from the company, rather than locals. They purportedly pay very high salaries and offer substantial benefits.

Religious schools

These schools follow a particular religious denomination. In these schools you will need to support and/or teach the religious curriculum in addition to the regular curriculum. Some of the hiring requirements may be strict and usually these schools will expect you to be a committed member of the faith in question. One colleague explained that, in her Catholic international school, you cannot be hired if you have had a child outside of marriage.

There are of course schools which are in these categories and do not match my descriptions, as well as schools that don't fit into any of these categories. If you search on the IB website, there are many schools which offer the IB throughout Europe, but does this make them 'international'? There are many 'mix and match' models therefore concrete descriptors are almost impossible to define.

In order to establish where your chosen international school best 'fits' within these general descriptors, you should carefully review the school website. It should detail how long a school has been established, the accreditations they may hold, and the curriculum followed. If you can access newsletters, which often are available on the school website, you can check if they are working towards accreditation. If you are still unsure, ask questions (as detailed in the previous chapter) following a successful interview to ensure you know the type of school, before you accept a contract. Research well and carefully, but if you are really struck on a location, you may need to compromise your top choice of school and vice versa. One international teacher explained:

> *"I knew that the school I was going to initially did not have a good reputation but it was my way into the country and so I risked it and came. I wish I had paid a bit more attention to the negative comments I had read but I managed to pull through the hard times and then another door opened and I got a job at one of the top schools in the country so it all worked out well in the end."*

CHAPTER 2

The Application Process

Finding a 'good fit'

This is probably the most important aspect of the job hunt. As you research a school, ask yourself: is this a place where I would be happy to live and work for at least two years? Keep in mind your personal key considerations and those listed in the previous chapter. Record each consideration in order of personal importance and match the schools with positions available to your list.

Creating a CV and cover letter

The application process will usually require a cover letter, personal statement, and/or completed application form. The school may require your personal statement to be a direct application for the role or a 'philosophy of education'.

Some schools may only request a CV and a cover letter.

In order to write an application, it is absolutely imperative at this stage that you:

> ➢ Find out everything you possibly can about the school – look through the website, check their newsletter and parents' guides (usually found on the website) and search their social media pages (Facebook, Twitter, LinkedIn and Instagram). Read everything ever written about the school, including published articles and if accredited, the accreditor's reports, which are often available on the school website or found through an internet search. It is as simple as using your preferred search engine and typing '(school name) inspection report'. As you read the reports, note areas in which you can support their ethos or improve their environment.

> ➢ Contact current or ex-teachers via Facebook, Twitter, and LinkedIn. Use these contacts to network and 'delve deeper' into the requirements of the school.

Questions to ask a teacher or on a forum:

(a) Did you feel supported transitioning to online learning (if applicable)?

(b) Do you still feel supported in your school?

(c) Are paperwork expectations and meetings manageable?

(d) When new initiatives are brought in, is training provided and is there time to consolidate each idea?

(e) Are the staff given a 'voice'? Are decisions which involve staff discussed with them?

(f) What is the resourcing like at the school?

(g) How is the staff supported with wellbeing? How is the morale at the school?

(h) Is there an expectation that emails/messages are answered and dealt with out-of-hours?

(i) Can you achieve a work/life balance?

(j) Would you recommend this school to a friend? Why/Why not?

(k) Is this a 'family school'? Is there provision or a crèche for staff children during training days?

(l) Is the salary reasonable for a family of....?

(m) Does the school make visa and permit requirements easy for staff and their families?

(n) Will it be easy for my partner to find work within/outside the school?

(o) What is the quality of healthcare like?

➢ Subscribe to view the comments about schools on 'The International School Review' (ISR) and the 'International School Advisor'. Each school is listed by region and you can access the reviews from ex-employees and employees. If there are several reviews, check for repeated opinions throughout the thread. However, if there are only one or two reviews, they can represent a one-sided viewpoint or reflect the opinion of a single disgruntled member/former member of staff. It is difficult to tell if this is the feeling of a few or many staff. In addition, be aware that comments may not be authentic and in fact could be written by anyone in the school (including the Senior Leadership Team).

As a subscriber to either of these sites, you can post on their forums asking about specific schools. Even if you are not a member, you can access and search the forum for information about a school. There is also a free forum for discussing schools, *staffroom.boards.net*, which you can access once registered. A further company, 'The International School Network', is currently in development and will allow teachers to connect and share peer reviews on international schools.

➢ Investigate the opinion of expats and/or parents whose children attend the school. You can search via Google, using terms such as '(name of school) parents' or 'living in (city)' which will often lead you to forums. You can also locate expats and family groups through a Facebook search using the country name and keywords such as 'international', 'expat', 'families', 'parents' and 'ladies'. Such groups are an invaluable resource for finding out about the school from the perspective of parents and the community.

➢ Research the management team. Their names and roles should be listed on the school website. You can find out more about the team on ISR, and by viewing their LinkedIn page (if you don't want this to be known, set your settings to anonymous) and other social media, such as Twitter and Instagram.

➢ Think about what hobbies and interests you wish to pursue. If it is important to you, investigate the community and charity work the school supports.

➢ Consider your own ethos and philosophy of education, and that will also help pinpoint aspects of the school which will suit you. For example:
  - do you enjoy inquiry-based learning?
  - do you want to teach a broad and balanced curriculum?
  - is a sports/arts curriculum focus important to you?
  - is a school which supports the community important?

If you can, visit the school. You can then experience first-hand how the school is run, and meet staff members and students.

Developing your CV

Remember, your CV is a marketing tool. Make it the best it can possibly be!

When you create your CV, make sure the content and style matches what the school is looking for. Schools list their 'Vision', 'Guiding Statement' and 'Learning Charters' on their website and on their documentation. Read these carefully and aim to match your CV to these as well as the job specification. For example, if the school values creating global citizens, list the clubs/activities you have led or currently lead, both inside and outside of school, which support this vision. Include any professional development you have received or led which could help develop the school or support their vision and mission.

Start with the barebone CV as described previously (see page 18). Next, include a short personal statement/career summary. This should be around three sentences, indicating in which country you were trained, your roles and your aspirations.

Then, you should begin by listing your work experience, reverse-chronologically. Ensure that there are no gaps and if there are, state why. Include both the month and the year. Next, use further subheadings for education, training courses attended (if you have attended many, list those most relevant to the application), plus activities you have run at the school, and/or voluntary work.

The CV should ideally be two pages, but no more than three pages in length. At the end of the CV, you can either state 'Referees to be provided upon request' or state your referees, which should all be, or almost all be, Headteachers. Begin with your current Head and do not only list colleagues.

By using clear formatting and sectioning on your CV, it will be easier to read, which is especially important if the school uses an Applicant Tracking System (ATS). As some schools receive huge numbers of applications, they may use this software to search for specific keywords and qualifications in order to ensure candidates match the job description. For example, if the application states that you must have 3+ years' experience and strong communication and proven managerial skills, the search will look for these keywords within your CV. If your CV does not match this basic list of requirements, it will be automatically discarded.

In a blog discussing how to develop a strong CV, Andrew Kurtuy explains that, in order to tailor your CV with keywords, you should look out for both job-related skills and action verbs. Job related skills are your primary characteristics and qualifications for the job, such as planning, teaching, and leading. Action verbs, such as 'created', 'pioneered', 'developed', etc. show what you have accomplished and how successful you have been in your job. After scanning the job description, list these words and develop your CV using them.

Furthermore, Kurtuy explains that in terms of format, PDF files are excellent at maintaining the design and formatting of your CV and, as they are universal, can be read by (most) ATS. However, he stresses that if the job application states that you must supply a Word document, this might mean that their ATS cannot read PDF files.

Cover letters and philosophy of education

As with the CV, should you be required to provide a cover letter or philosophy of education, ensure you carefully review the school 'mission', advert, and job specification and make a list of the qualities the school is seeking. Wherever you can, match these qualities with actual examples within your cover letter/philosophy of education. Again, use the knowledge from your research to ensure you *sell yourself* so the school will feel you are a good match and that you will improve the school by being part of it.

At this point you can discuss 'deficits' within the school and state that you have noticed these and what your solution would be. For example, you may state that after researching the school you can see that they are adopting 1:1 provision of technology. Here you could state that this transition is often challenging for x, y, and z reasons but that you have 'x' years' experience supporting this in terms of training staff and children. Therefore, you are providing a solution to a problem they may already have or are likely to encounter soon.

Aim to be succinct and create a letter of maximum two pages. Again, *prove* how you match the requirements by *what you have done*, with concrete examples. But above all, be honest. A Head of Key Stage 1 explains:

> *"From an employer's point of view, friendly, happy people who only put 'factuals' on their CV are what I look for; whereas glowing it up with lots of superlatives or copying text from the government website makes me worried."*

Begin your cover letter with a short summary of your teaching career to date including any significant further education, as illustrated in the following example:

> I feel I am suited this role as I exceed the required criteria as a fully qualified UK teacher with QTS, with the induction period completed in the UK. My teaching career post-qualification includes two years in the UK and a further nine years' experience within British international schools implementing the National Curriculum for England, the Early Years Foundation Stage framework, and the International Primary Curriculum. In order to advance my knowledge of pedagogy, I recently completed a Masters in Early Years education. This knowledge, and my strong connections within the local community, enabled me to create and develop my own successful Early Years business. Managing my own business with parents as partners was a natural progression in my career development.

Then tailor the letter to the needs of the school. Here is an extract from a cover letter where collaboration and community were a key aspect of the school:

> I contribute to the wider school by helping establish a strong sense of community. I enjoy leading extra-curricular activities with children of

other classes to establish myself within the school and to get to know a wider range of pupils. Further, in several schools, I have developed in-school links with Primary and Foundation Stage, through a Year 6 shared/guided reading programme, Year 1 transition, and regularly working with other year groups for reading and special events.

In my first international posting, I created a house points system with regular 'team' events for the whole of EYFS, which was comprised of sixteen classes. This was highly successful and was used as a whole unit reward system. Within my own class, I encourage children to work in pairs and small groups often. Such collaboration within the class and school raises the confidence of all parties involved and the children develop a sense of responsibility for one another. Within an international context, building such a community is important as children may not experience the extended networks they would do at home.

Similarly, parents need to feel welcome within the school so they also feel part of the school community. I have a friendly, approachable manner and I encourage parents to partake in class events and share their knowledge. Two-way conversation and feedback are important to me, so I regularly connect with parents through the school's communication system, Seesaw.

Another example, this time an application to a school whose mission was to create reflective thinkers, note the direct quote of one of the school's guiding principles:

As reflective thinkers, it is important that children discuss and celebrate cultural similarities and differences. I support your guiding principle of 'leaving people and places in a better state than when you found them' through developing a sense of responsibility and open-mindedness in children. My goal is to create globally responsible citizens, who are accepting of cultures and societies different to their own. An example from my own practice included a discussion after a local area walk which raised awareness of privilege and inequality within our own society. We then raised money through a sponsored walk and as part of a Christmas event for those less fortunate, including a local orphanage.

In addition, support your application by showing you are aware of the school's standing, reputation, and how you will fit in easily to the environment:

I am motivated to apply to (...) school, as it provides excellent facilities and is accredited by both the Council of International Schools (CIS) and the Western Association of Schools and Colleges (WASC). Further, your school is highly recommended by international teachers. Therefore, I am assured that my workplace will involve sound academic policies and practice, with a commitment to excellence. In addition, I am very interested in the collaborative environment of your EYFS unit. I feel I could share my experience and ideas to support other teachers within the team. I am also keen to live in Asia, within a country which supports an eco-friendly mindset, offering better access to outdoor green spaces and with less pollution compared to other Asian cities.

International schools look to recruit teachers who are independent and adaptable, who have a good grasp of their curriculum and are used to working in environments similar to theirs. Therefore, if you have experience within private education, schools with EAL children, or working with children requiring learning support, discuss these experiences. Ensure that you state how you have succeeded in these environments and raised levels of attainment for these children. A Headteacher provides this perfect summary:

> *"When talking about your experience of teaching, [the employer] should be able to see that you have an understanding [of the role], and [the application should be] personalised so they can visualise you in the role. Some teachers just copy (I kid you not) the same blurb under each position they have had!"*

Providing documentation

Keep a record of the schools you apply to, the date of application, and the closing date. You could add this to the spreadsheet of schools created during your research. Regularly check this list to follow up on applications. If you have not heard approximately one week after the closing date, follow up with an email asking if your application has been received. Let the school know you are still actively interested in the position and are available for any further questions.

If you are a first-time international teacher, it is highly likely that you will need to apply to many schools before getting an interview. If you are rejected by schools, politely request feedback. Use this feedback to adapt subsequent applications.

When you do receive an interview request, keep a copy of your application to refer to during the interview. Additionally, you can keep this as a good example should you need to apply to subsequent schools.

Interviews

Generally speaking, you will need to complete one or two interviews with a school to secure a role. This will be through a recruitment fair, which could be online or in-person, or an online interview through Skype or another platform. If you are in the same country, you may have a face-to-face interview.

A school may expect you to visit for an interview or to teach a lesson. If you use a recruitment agency, you may just interview once with the agency, but it is still quite likely that schools would want to interview you also.

Here are some ways in which you may be interviewed:

1. Attending a recruitment fair: These events are often organised by recruitment companies, either in person or online. Often a full list of schools attending will be published beforehand, so before considering a fair, it is important to ensure there are several schools attending in which you would like to work. In most cases, after successfully completing an interview(s) you will be informed quickly whether you have been accepted for the position or not.

'In person' fairs typically follow this format:

> ➤ The candidate applies for the fair. If this is a joint application, then include your partner's details also.
> ➤ An invite will be sent by the agency or recruiting organisation. The venue could be a conference centre or hotel.
> ➤ Typically, as a candidate, you will be able to view different school teams by presenting yourself at their 'booth'. You may register your interest for roles which they have.

> ➤ As the day progresses, schools send invites for interviews via a personal mailbox. These may include schools which you may not have considered.
> ➤ You can attend general meetings about working in different countries and school-specific meetings, where you can learn more about a school and often ask questions of the recruiter/leadership team.
> ➤ If you do secure interviews, these will be done within the building itself. If you are successful, the school will notify you after the event.

2. Attending a recruitment event organised by an umbrella company: Typically, these will be based within a conference centre or hotel. These take place after you have expressed an interest in a school or completed the application process.

> ➤ An umbrella company may give a presentation about their schools.
> ➤ Separate interviews will take place with schools in which you show an interest (or vice versa).
> ➤ The candidate is either told at interview or contacted later if they are successful.

I have attended recruitment events such as these twice in my career. At both it was lovely to meet the Heads in person and have my questions answered about the schools.

3. Attending a school tour: If you are serious about a school, it is a good idea to request a school tour. This shows commitment and will give you a chance to impress the Headteacher and other staff. Furthermore, this is a solid opportunity to decide whether the school is a good fit for yourself, partner, and family. Some schools may request

that you visit a school for the interview. Depending on the requirements, the school may request you to teach a lesson or to be interviewed by children, so be prepared for this possible eventuality.

If you are interviewed after the visit, you can discuss your experience, mentioning the positives and also where you could support improvement within the school. On the other hand, after a tour you may decide against working at the school. You can be upfront and decline the interview.

On my third international move, I had made an application to a school and I asked if I could visit to ensure my family were a good fit. I got a good feel for the school. I had a great conversation with the management. I felt this experience really supported my application and I got the job!

4. Skype interviews: This is by far the most common method for international schools to interview candidates. The advantages of video interviews include the ability to be in your own space. A disadvantage of these interviews includes the lack of face-to-face contact and the unreliability of technology! This is unlikely to affect you in the UK, however should you interview in a country with poor Internet connections, this can be very stressful.

When in a video interview, remember to smile and express as much of your personality as possible. This is easier to convey in person, so show your 'best self' – ensure you are upbeat, confident, and knowledgeable.

Have a few questions prepared to show that you have researched the school well. Further, during the interview you can have a list of key words/comments you wish to mention in the interview within view (placed at the left or right of the screen so you do not need to look down).

Ensure that you sell yourself, as you would in a CV, as this is your chance to convince the interviewers that they need you at their school. Look professional and dress exactly as you would for a face-to-face interview. Make sure you sit in front of an appropriate background, check your microphone and camera, and adjust your seating before the interview commences.

Top Tip

If you are interviewing as a couple, you can listen to your partner's interview to give yourself an understanding of the kind of questions you may be asked.

Interview questions

Here are some questions you may be asked, and it is a good idea to prepare responses prior to the interview. If possible, practice the interview with a friend or colleague beforehand. When practicing in this way, ask the interviewer to provide feedback on your answers.

(a) Tell me about your career to date.
(b) Why do you want to work at our school?
(c) What would a typical day in your class look like? What would I see if I came into your classroom?
(d) Tell me about your best lesson.
(e) How do you engage learners overall? Special Support/EAL learners?
(f) How do you support learners with Special Educational Needs or are EAL?
(g) Where do you see yourself in the future?
(h) What can you bring to our school?
(i) Do you work well in a team? Give me an example.

(j) Tell me about a negative experience within school and how you dealt with it.

(k) Have you ever worked with difficult people? How did you manage that?

(l) What would you say is your worst quality?

(m) How do you think your family would adapt? Would your partner be looking to work?

(n) Would you need to return to the UK for any reason?

(o) Tell us what you have done outside of class to support the school, for example, coaching or developing an area of the school?

(p) How did you adapt to online teaching? What tools are you using?

(q) How do you use data?

(r) Give examples of your use of teaching assistants.

(s) How would you deal with (example provided) safeguarding concern?

(t) Give examples of differentiation within your class.

(u) If your friends or colleagues had to describe you in three words, what would they say?

Top tips

Prior to the interview, read through all the documentation you have sent to the school, as your questions will be based on these. Look again through the school website, Twitter feeds and other social media, noting the most current events which you could discuss. In addition, research the local culture so you can show that you have explored this area. If you know the school will be going through an accreditation, read up about the accreditation company in advance.

At interview, try to remain calm when asked questions and give yourself time to think. If you are unsure of what you are being asked, or need more time, ask the interviewer to repeat the question or rephrase it. As they do this, map out a reply. Try to use keywords that reflect what the school is looking for (as outlined in their specification). As with the covering letter and CV, ensure you discuss how you are skilled in a certain area, and provide examples to back it up. Often international schools look for recent and relevant UK experience, in order to support latest best practice in the UK and training. If appropriate, discuss the most recent training you have had, ensuring you stipulate how it was applied in your classroom. The interview is not a time to be humble but to share all *relevant* personal and work-based achievements you have made whilst in your current and previous schools.

It is important you do not just list all your accomplishments. Listen carefully to the interviewer and answer the question they ask. Show enthusiasm for information the interviewer shares and you can ask further questions to clarify what they share with you. Be yourself and remember that interviews are always a two-way discussion.

Be mindful that the interview is not the time to discuss or negotiate salary. If you are unsure about any salary/benefit information, this can be discussed after an offer is made.

Questions to ask a school

Upon conclusion of an interview, the interviewer will ask if you have any questions. Below is a checklist of key areas that are wise to know about in advance of a move. In the interview, limit your questions to two or three related to teaching and learning. Send any benefits and package questions to HR before accepting a contract.

Suggested questions to ask at interview

(a) Your website states that your teaching and learning supports (child-led learning/academic emphasis/developing the whole child). What are the outcomes of this? How would I see this in your school?

(b) What is the current focus of the school?

(c) What Personal Development opportunities do your staff take part in?

(d) Does your school work with any charities or local organisations? Are children involved in this too?

(e) What does your Diversity, Equality and Inclusion program look like? How are students involved in this?

(f) Is student voice important?

(g) What does assessment look like in the school?

(h) What are the standards of behaviour?

(i) How is the school resourced for learning materials?

(j) What is your staff retention like? What do staff leave to do next?

(k) Are there opportunities for promotion?

(l) What are the demographics of the school and the language background of pupils and staff?

Suggested questions to direct to HR

(a) How has the school dealt with the pandemic/political unrest/earthquakes (any concern here) in your school? What precautions have you implemented? How are/were teachers supported?

(b) What are the requirements in terms of extra-curricular activities, meetings outside of contracted hours, weekend work?

(c) How many hours are non-contact time and duties?

(d) How does the school support teachers and their families? Is childcare provided during inset and out-of-hours work? Does the school have crèche facilities (for younger children)?

(e) Where do teachers live?

(f) What kind of healthcare insurance is provided?

(g) Are there school and community events? Is there a staff book club/football team/hiking group (insert interest here)?

(h) What activities are available in the local area?

(i) What are the benefits, such as housing, flights, and pension?

Salary and benefits

The salary and benefits of international schools can vary widely. As of 2021, the countries known to offer the highest salary plus benefit packages are China, Saudi Arabia, Hong Kong, and Kuwait.

However, other countries can offer great salaries relative to the cost of living. Prior to an interview, research the current salary expectations of international teachers within the country/city. This is easy to do, as there are forums and blogs where teachers discuss this, such as ISR and ISN. Also use a Google search of 'international teacher salary in (…)' to see if there are examples available. Investigate whether this would be a comfortable wage for you to live on and what teachers are able to save on your salary (if this is a necessity for you).

Further, check the website 'numbeo'. On this site you can compare the cost of living with other countries, such as your home country. When you work out the figures, combined with the other benefits, you should be able to decide how much you would need to live on and how much you could save.

Some schools have a fixed salary scale, much like the UK, but others do not. If you are not provided with a salary from a published scale, it may be open to negotiation. Negotiating is advisable, particularly if you feel the salary seems lower than the earnings of other teachers working in the region, or if you are an experienced teacher with a good deal to offer. Should you decide to negotiate the salary, state your reasons, such as dependents you need to support or the offer being lower than your current salary.

Some packages include payment of in-country taxes. If your tax is not paid, check the rate! This may drastically reduce your salary, especially in European countries where the rate can be high.

Both you and your dependents should be covered by health insurance too. Some schools require you to pay a percentage of the cost of the health insurance package. Check the level of cover carefully and clarify any issues you may foresee. If you have a pre-existing medical condition, it is important that you notify the insurance company and find out what you may need to pay, or you may not be covered at all. Most schools' group insurance will cover pre-existing conditions, but it is always better to check.

An international teacher's package can include housing allowance. This is a set amount used to pay your rent every month. As some countries demand large deposits, often known as 'key money' (notably Korea and Japan), your school may also offer to pay this or at least lend you the money when you arrive. The allowance can be provided as part of your pay check and paid into your bank account, or it may be paid directly to the landlord. Some schools only offer the latter. If you have a choice, request that you pay the landlord; that way, you may be able to choose a property that rents for less than the allowance and you can pocket the extra money. However, some schools, especially those in Europe, do not provide this allowance.

It is worth comparing the housing allowance specified with the rental costs near to the school. To do this, research local real estate companies or email them directly, questioning what would be available within that price bracket. Also, check the allowance if you are married, a teaching couple, or have children. In these cases, the rental allowance should be higher. Some of the better packages, especially within the UAE, will also pay utilities. This is another area to check when considering a package. A further option is that the school provides housing for you and you do not receive a housing allowance.

Housing allowances can vary considerably between schools. One school did not change the allowance for more than seven years, and our two-bedroom apartment cost around double our monthly housing allowance. Comparatively, in a different school when renting a larger apartment, I paid less than the allowance. Generally speaking, in South East Asia, I have found that the more 'modern' or 'westernised' the property and/or building is, the higher the rental cost.

If you have children, confirm if the cost of their place within the school is fully or partially covered. Most schools cover tuition for up to two children, so if you have more than this you need to ask whether they will receive free tuition. The cost of tuition added to your package can increase the value of the package significantly. In addition, check that both health and accident insurance are in place for your children.

Further, it would also be pertinent to ask the school if contract extensions are offered should both parties agree to it. This is an important consideration, especially if you have dependents, as you may wish to stay at a school longer than the initial contract period. Being granted just a two-year contract with no option for renewal may be less appealing to those wishing to settle in a location longer term.

Many schools offer a beginning and end of contract flight, for yourself and your dependents. The 'better' packages offer flights every year. You will either have the flights booked for you, or an amount paid into your bank account relative to the cost of economy return flights. When given the option, if the allowance is acceptable, choose the latter. This means you are not tied to a trip home and instead you can use this money for flights to other destinations, giving you some flexibility.

Finally, some schools offer a relocation and repatriation package as a specified lump sum. A relocation allowance financially supports teachers to ship furniture and keepsakes to the country, or with buying household goods. The remuneration for this will often vary depending on whether your family includes a partner and children. A repatriation package can be used when you leave the school to pay for shipping and any fees associated with your next destination.

International schools often offer a '13th' month bonus as part of your salary. This is paid every year if you complete the entire school year. The idea behind this is that it is approximately the amount you would receive per year as a pension. In the Middle East, it is quite common to receive an increasing bonus for every year that you complete, thereby providing an incentive to stay.

As a guideline, depending on location, expect to receive a similar or higher wage as a UK teacher, pre-tax. The school should pay for at least a proportion of your health insurance. Further, the housing allowance ought to cover a minimum of one bedroom per member of your family in a reasonable area, within 15 minutes commute of the school. Depending on location, you should also expect flights home for yourself and your dependents, especially if both you and your partner are employed by the school.

In my career to date, my best overall package was in a large not-for-profit school which had substantial fees. However, in my first international placement, I took much less than my ideal but I gained valuable experience and it was a truly happy workplace for me.

Salary and benefits should not be your most significant consideration, unless you have major debt to pay off. In addition to this, consider the package as a whole: the country, lifestyle, cost of living, school, your potential colleagues and if applicable, the quality of education for your child(ren) and opportunities for trailing spouses.

Another consideration which will affect a salary package is the size of the school and class sizes. A smaller school will be unable to offer a large salary. The location of the school also plays a part. It is understood that schools in more enviable locations, such as tropical islands and practically anywhere in Europe, will offer a lower salary and less in terms of benefits. International schools based in European countries do not usually offer an 'expat package' but are more akin to what you would expect in your home country. They are not likely to pay for any flights, housing, or insurance.

In addition, in a less developed country, the salary offered may not be substantial due to the cost of living. However, if you are looking to save money, investigate schools in countries that are considered 'hardship locations' for expats. Hardship locations usually offer increased salaries with greater benefits because the country may offer less amenities, poor travel connections and/or a challenging environment for some.

However, be aware that your own lifestyle expectations can affect how impressive a package may be in reality. Living frugally and eating locally will obviously be more cost effective than holidays in premium locations and dining in expensive restaurants. Most importantly, make sure you research the cost of living, especially housing, when you receive your contract proposal.

The offer

After interviewing successfully, you will usually be contacted within a few days, by email or phone, with a job offer.

At this stage, the salary and benefits will be outlined in brief. Should you feel the offer is not reasonable, you can negotiate. If you are happy with the suggested salary and benefits, you then agree to provisionally accept the offer as long as the contract upholds all that has been stipulated. You can stall a little at this stage if the offer is something you need to consider, but schools prefer a decision straight away, or after a short time period.

If you accept, schools see this acceptance as a commitment from you, so unless the contract is very different from the offer, you will be expected to sign when it is received. Once you receive the contract, check it thoroughly. If you have any questions, email these directly to HR.

Other considerations

Often teachers seek a school where they will feel 'happy'. The demographic of the teacher greatly influences where they feel the happiest. For example, those with young children look for a safe environment and an abundance of activities for children. They will seek 'family-friendly' schools which offer facilities such as a crèche. Conversely, this is less important to young, single teachers. This demographic is more likely to seek opportunities for great nightlife and restaurants. They are likely to want to live in, or near to, a transport hub offering opportunities for extensive travel. However, with many other considerations also playing a part, it would appear that the perfect location and the perfect school are very specific to each individual.

Every school reflects the staff, management, and overall community, at any given time. Unfortunately, staff and situations in international schools usually change frequently. A school can be considered very desirable one year, but the following year the perception can be quite different. For example, a school's management style may completely change when the management prioritise efficiency, monitoring, and being professional and/or corporate. Teachers can be expected to be more like salespeople, available to stop their lesson and 'sell' their school when parents come to visit. Further, if a school emphasises its 'look', aspiring to be like the 'big' corporate schools such as 'Dulwich' or 'Harrow', it may demand that creative displays and teaching styles become more standardised. Sometimes the larger and more corporate a school, the less teachers feel supported, and therefore morale decreases. Conversely, smaller schools often offer a more personal experience.

Similarly, some schools offer greater support to their teachers with wellbeing programmes and more realistic expectations for workload than others. As you consider a school, check their website for wellbeing initiatives and seek out current or ex-teachers' opinions.

As stated previously, seek a school which matches your educational philosophy and adheres to it in all they do. That way, it is likely the teachers you will work with will also follow this ethos. Being on the same page will enable you to establish friendships with like-minded teachers and to 'fit in'.

It is true that a 'happy' environment is often one where teachers feel settled. Prior to accepting a position, it is worthwhile looking into the expat communities within the location you are considering. Some places, such as Singapore, Bangkok, and Hong Kong, have thriving communities which offer a range of activities and support. Other countries, such as Taiwan, have much smaller expat communities, meaning that you have to put more effort into finding friends and activities that suit you. Researching expat groups online, through Facebook groups, Google searches, and other forums should shed light on the expat communities of particular locations you are interested in. Use keywords in your search, such as 'Parents in (insert country)', '(Country name) families', '(Country name) ladies', 'Living in (Country name)'.

Once you have accepted a job offer, it is worth learning the basics of the host country's language before you get there, as this can ease your transition somewhat. It is a great feeling to be able to connect not just with other expats but also with the local population. The ability to communicate in your host country, even at the most basic level, can also foster a sense of wellbeing and happiness, and even reduce stress.

During the Covid-19 pandemic, many schools around the world were forced to close and adopt online learning. When deciding on a workplace, it is worth bearing in mind how staff were treated in response to the crisis. Check through the website and ask former/current teachers what the school did in terms of precautions and support for teachers transitioning to online learning. How a school dealt with the pandemic can be a measure of how staff are supported in a more general way.

I feel a 'happy' school is where staff feel they are compensated enough and they enjoy a good work/life balance. Wellbeing and professional development should be a focus and the school would have a low staff turnover. Teachers should be encouraged to pursue their interests and given support in achieving their goals. Further, I feel an ideal school should offer a democratic environment, where new initiatives are shared and discussed. The feeling within the school should be positive for both students and staff.

CHAPTER 3

Preparations

As you consider what you need to do for the move, request a 'buddy' from the school to answer questions for you. This may not be a colleague within your team, but ideally someone matched to your circumstances; for example, a single teacher, a colleague with a young family, or a teaching couple. Ideally, they should be able to offer you support and advice on very specific questions, thereby eliminating the need to send multiple questions to HR (who may not be able to relate to your specific circumstances).

Visas and authentication of documents

Once you accept a job at an international school, you will receive your contract, usually by post, to sign. When you return the contract, the school will provide information on your next steps.

It is extremely important to read through the document requirements from HR carefully, especially in reference to processing your work visa. The requirements for a visa vary from country to country and can change frequently due to government changes in policy. Therefore, below details a brief overview of what is often expected, but be aware that this is only a guide.

The school should provide you with all the details on what they need in order to attain a work/residence permit for you. In general, schools usually ask for a copy of your passport, degree certificate, teaching credentials, passport photos, police check, marriage certificate (if applicable), and your child/children's birth certificate (if applicable) to be authenticated and notarised.

If this is your first move from your home country, both authentication and notarisation should be done in your country before you leave. The authentication is usually done at a consulate of the country you are applying to move to, whilst the notarisation can be completed by a solicitor. There are several solicitors in the UK that will do this all through the post, so either for convenience or if you already live abroad, you can use this service for your authenticated documents. If you do, ensure you track the package either by DHL or another signed for/recorded method. Alternatively, the HR department of your new school should be able to offer details of a visa agency to take care of all this for you – the authentication and notarisation. This is a very convenient option, but it is often expensive.

Preparing your documents is your responsibility and, should they not be ready in time, will impact your ability to work legally. As it can take several months, start this process as soon as possible.

In addition to notarised documents, the school's HR department will provide you with further instructions of what may be necessary for your application for a work visa/residence permit. Different schools have different requirements, but you should expect full support with this process. It is likely you will need to complete a medical test and will be required to visit the relevant country consulate. If you should need to visit a government office, ensure you bring extra photocopies of all your documents, plus spare photos, a pen, glue, and scissors.

My transition to Egypt was relatively easy as I was able to visit a consulate in London but when moving to Taiwan from Vietnam, the process was far more complicated. On the Vietnamese side, the consulate demanded a full medical to issue a visa, whilst I was told on the Taiwan side (from my school) that this was not necessary. It was just a bureaucratic add-on! Yet you need to follow the rules of the country you are based in.

Schools usually reimburse all costs relating to visas, but this is something you should confirm when discussing a contract. Keep all of your receipts plus a copy of each.

Finally, you will need to complete a criminal record check. Currently, for UK citizens, checks are issued by the Disclosure and Barring Service (DBS), a Home Office-sponsored public group. You are likely to already have one if you have recently taught or are teaching in the UK. If you currently teach outside of the UK you must provide a criminal check to the DBS service, usually issued by the police from your resident country. DBS checks cover a period of five years preceding your application. In addition to police checks covering that time period, you are required to submit the addresses of each residence in which you have lived.

Shipping

Another consideration is whether to ship your belongings (including furniture) or to purchase items when you arrive. Make sure you check whether you will receive a shipping allowance paid by the school or not. In addition, check the availability of both furnished/unfurnished property. If you ship furniture, you will need to concentrate on renting unfurnished properties.

Choosing not to ship

A furnished apartment may make sense initially. If you purchase extra baggage allowance for your flight, you can have your most important belongings available immediately to help you settle. Furthermore, this inevitably reduces the cost of the move compared to shipping, which can be very expensive. If you receive a relocation allowance you can instead use this to buy new items when you arrive.

A disadvantage of not shipping is trying to manage all of your luggage when you arrive. It is a good idea to make the school aware of this situation and ask for support upon arrival. Ensure that you have a safe place to store your possessions until you find somewhere to live.

Shipping goods

The options here are either to ship by air or sea freight. You will be able to move the bulk of your belongings all at once and have less to worry about in terms of furnishing when you arrive. Whichever method you choose, you should speak to several shipping companies to compare services and prices.

By Sea

It will be necessary to arrange this far in advance of the move. You will need to ensure there is an appropriate place to receive your shipping. Some shippers require that you ship a whole container (or you pay for a whole one no matter what you ship). This is something to be aware of and to discuss with the shipping company.

By Air

This is a great option if you need to keep your belongings with you right up to the move, or, if you only have a small amount to ship. As air freight takes much less time, you can receive it promptly after arrival. However, this method of shipping is much more expensive than sea freight.

You can also use a mixture of both excess luggage and shipping. This way all your most important belongings can be taken with you as baggage, whilst your shipping could come later, after you have found a place to live.

However, you need to research your shipping options early as, depending on where you are moving to and the method you choose, the shipment can take weeks to arrive. In addition, some countries will not let you import your shipment until you have entered the country and/or have your visa. This means you can end up having to wait for your shipment and there can be additional charges for storage if there is a delay in the visa when you arrive. Try to plan your shipment accordingly. Research carefully any restrictions on what goods/texts are not allowed to avoid any complications with customs.

When teachers were asked about reputable companies for shipping, there was a general agreement that the credibility of the local office at your departure point may be more important than the brand. Therefore, research this well and check how their service measures up internationally. Furthermore, check if the shipper has offices in both your arrival and departure countries, or whether they use a different firm. This could adversely affect the experience at the destination point. As each experience of shipping is highly personal, it is very hard to rank them. However, below is a list of recommended companies listed by teachers, in no particular order:

Seven Seas, AGS, Asian Tigers, Santa Fe Relocators, Allied Pickfords, Yamato (Japan), Crown Shipping, Send my Bag.

Overall, I would recommend that you ask your school buddy/HR or research local Facebook groups about the preferred shippers that expats use to your destination.

After you have booked your flights, ensure you supply HR with all the details. It is worth comparing different routes via Skyscanner or a similar app, as prices can vary greatly depending on how many stops you take, for example.

In all my moves, I have bought extra baggage for the flight. I have done this for simplicity and the fact that I have never bought extensive furniture that I wished to keep. Prior to moving, I sold/gave away all of my furniture and household goods before leaving. You can offer these on classifieds, through Facebook groups, or to colleagues.

Personal preparations

After organizing your documentation, shipping requirements, and flights, it is a good idea to set your affairs in order before you travel. Here are some useful suggestions:

1. *Banking*: you may wish to inform your bank that you are moving abroad for a short period and ask if they can offer credit cards which do not charge for purchases abroad or withdrawals from abroad. You may want to check your current account conditions, as some accounts require you to be a resident of the UK. Sharing this information will also stop the banks locking accounts, which happens (especially in the case of VISA/Mastercard) when many purchases are made from aboard. Further, ensure you have set up online banking so you can check your accounts from abroad. You should also set up telephone banking in case there is an urgent issue. It is important, where possible, to keep at least one account open so that you can transfer your earnings.

2. *Vaccinations*: check with your travel clinic/nurse which vaccinations you will require well ahead of time. Some vaccinations require several shots, weeks apart. If you'd like

to check for yourself, the 'travel health pro' website has a list of vaccinations required for each country, in addition to other risks such as malaria. When you move overseas, bring a copy of vaccination records for yourself and your dependents.

3. *Savings*: ensure you bring enough money with you to live comfortably for up to two months, as well as extra cash to allow you to buy furniture and household goods. If you are due to receive a relocation stipend, this will likely be unavailable immediately. You could be waiting a month or more for your first salary and this allowance. It is a good idea to check this directly with HR.

4. *Cancel any direct debits for things you don't need whilst abroad*: this can include TV license payment, internet subscriptions, phone contracts, any child benefit you receive, etc. It is likely that this will be far more difficult from abroad.

5. *Health:* if you have any pre-existing health conditions, or you know that you may be susceptible to mental health issues, it is vital you check the availability of medication you need and support services in your host country prior to a move. To travel with certain medicines, you may need a medical certificate, so research this carefully.

6. *Take photocopies and/or digital copies of documents*: keep a copy both digitally and hard copy of *all* important documents, such as your passport, certifications, visas, driving licenses, and bank/credit cards just in case anything should go missing. You can take photos of these documents and securely save them online. Check the expiry dates on these important documents and renew any which are close to expiry.

7. *Bring passport photos*: bring at least 10 recent passport photos of yourself and your dependents. You can usually get these whilst abroad but having them readily available

reduces the stress of seeking a shop or service when you just arrive.

8. *Keep a UK residential address:* this will allow you to have a place where post can be received, and ideally also checked by a trusted person. When important items such as your bank account cards expire, you need a safe place to send them to. This is also important especially when hiring a car in the UK and you need recent bank statements to prove your address.

9. *Organise any held property:* if you have a property, ensure you have someone who can support the running of this, or you can pay an agency to manage it. You may well need to pay taxes on property as capital gains.

10. *Returned tax:* should you be based in the UK and relocating abroad, inform the tax office immediately when you finish work by sending in your p45. You will then receive back any tax owed after it is calculated in April.

11. *National Insurance contributions:* should you wish to retire in the UK, it makes sense to continue paying your National Insurance contributions. Whilst at home, you can declare you are moving abroad or you can do this from abroad, once you send your details of overseas work. You can pay these retrospectively, up to 10 years. Ask for Class 2 contributions as you will work abroad. These are substantially lower than the full fee.

12. *Teachers' Pension:* if you have this pension or any other pension in the UK, make sure you talk to a financial advisor or the organisation to inform them of your move abroad, and what the consequences may be, if any.

13. *Create a will:* this is usually done through a solicitor and will take around two weeks to finalise after the initial discussion. It is wise to ensure that, should anything happen, there are clear instructions for the allocation of your assets.

14. *Set an emergency contact:* should you have any problems in your new school, such as a medical problem or an

unforeseen emergency, you need someone at home who can support you.

Also make sure that you:

Visit friends and family: see everyone you can! This seems obvious, but it can be the hardest part of leaving, so do not avoid it. Instead, plan regular (video) calls and commit to instant messaging, or however you usually communicate.

Pack your 'creature comforts': if your shipping allowance allows, pick out your favourite snacks/spices/foods to pack, as well as other essentials which will make you feel more 'at home' when abroad. In order to find out what is available in your host country, ask on a Facebook page/group (which you should have already joined) for that country. Also, find out what local supermarkets there are and see if they stock what you need. Often an online search will show the supermarkets and also their produce.

CHAPTER 4

Arrival

The school should offer airport pickup for you and a contact immediately on arrival. If they do not, request a contact and the best way to reach your location from the airport. Arriving in a new country can be disorientating, so the less stress you experience the better. Some schools strive to support their new arrivals, as one teacher describes:

> *"The school was great when we first arrived. They collected us from the airport and took us to our apartment and gave us a sim card and things such as kitchen stuff and bedding to set us up. This initial start helped to alleviate my worries about where I'd live and what I'd do on my first night without anything in the flat."*

Often when you arrive at the airport, you can buy a cheap 'tourist sim', with several weeks of phone credit/WIFI. This will allow you to be connected quickly to both contacts at home and necessary new contacts abroad, such as your housing agent.

Your next priority will be either moving into, or searching for, suitable housing. There may be a pack ready to support your transition and quite likely a schedule of social events before induction starts.

Housing

School provided housing: you may be required to move into a school-owned apartment, either on-site or close to the school. This is reasonable especially when the school is part of one large site which is not located close to other amenities, or is a boarding school where you may be required to commit to other duties in the evenings and/or at weekends. Request HR to send you some pictures of your new home so you can have an idea of what to bring or ship. You may also be able to request an inventory list so that you can budget for purchases upon arrival.

Often living in school apartments can be a short term (one year) option, therefore you can move out after a year and receive an allowance instead. For the first year, living in school-owned property is a very convenient option, as you do not need to complete a housing search initially, and often these residences are fully furnished. Therefore, you only need to buy personal items such as towels, pans, and small items. However, one trailing spouse, who did not have a choice over housing, warned:

> *"...our school in Qatar (and this is quite common in the Middle East) provided apartments within an apartment block and all teachers lived there, apart from senior management staff, who were provided with houses on compounds. In both cases, there was no choice but to live in the housing provided. This can cause problems, for example if the apartments are not in good neighbourhoods, the villas are not on nice compounds, or singles are mixed with families..."*

School completes a search of rental properties: a school may offer, or insist upon, picking out properties for you and send you photos/ videos to help support your decision. These properties may have had teachers living there previously or are properties which are well known to the school. You may have the opportunity to buy furniture from the previous tenant. This can be an excellent option, especially for the first move abroad. Finding a property when you just arrive can be stressful and difficult if you are not clear on what you are looking for, which areas are best to live in, or what a reasonable rental price is.

Renting an apartment you select: one advantage of renting your own apartment is that you can choose the area in which you live, which may be more private and further removed from other teachers and/ or parents of the children you teach. This scenario usually involves arriving in the country and staying in a hotel whilst you search for a property.

HR should provide a list of housing agents but it is also worthwhile seeking your own agents and recommendations. Prior to relocating, email several agents photos of the type of apartment you are seeking, as well as a 'must have' list for the apartment, such as number of bedrooms and amenities. Set a price range or the maximum rental you would like to pay per month. If you can avoid it, it is better not to declare your allowance, as agencies are likely to only show you properties which match this.

Ask your school buddy about the preferred residential areas and the range that you can expect to pay for your requirements. In addition, look at real estate websites online for the range of properties you will be able to afford, along with the average rental prices per month, or check agents' windows once you move.

When viewing properties, ask the agent for the details of each apartment to be written down and make sure you bring your phone/camera to take photos of each apartment you see, including the front door with the address on. After viewing more than five properties it can be very easy to mix them up!

Once you find a property you like, re-visit it on a different day, resisting any pressure from the agent. Agents are likely to spin half-truths such as 'your colleague is interested', etc. If you do like a property, ensure you check out the transport links (especially the links to school). Check the environment of the property both during the day and the evening. If you need a quiet space to return home to, check that this is the case in the evening and at weekends also.

Furnished housing: moving directly into a fully furnished apartment can often be the easiest option. Unless you are able buy all your furniture from a leaving teacher, you can save money by not purchasing furniture. As you adapt to your new surroundings, finding furniture can be a huge hassle on top of all the other jobs you need to complete. At the bare minimum, request white goods (refrigerator, freezer, washing machine). These are generally the most expensive items to buy. Should there be any issue with these items during your tenancy, providing it is not just general wear and tear, the landlord will be likely to repair or replace them (check your housing contract carefully to ensure this).

Unfurnished housing: the advantage of this is that you can kit your home out how you like it. This may be the only choice if you decide to ship your furniture. Often, unfurnished properties are cheaper. On the flip side, if you see a furnished apartment that you really like, the landlord is unlikely to want to remove the furniture.

If you are moving with a partner, check that your property will also suit their needs, should they wish to work or stay at home. This is explored in greater depth in Chapter 6.

Once you have spent some time in your new location, if you are unhappy with the property, it is often fairly easy to move. In terms of agents, you can follow up recommendations from colleagues or take on property as colleagues leave. You will know what to include in a rental contract, exactly the areas you want to live, and the price range you should expect to pay.

Viewing properties is often a tedious process: you will quickly notice if the agent actually knows their properties or not. Some agents will show you many unsuitable properties, then finish the viewings with a property at the end of the day that perhaps didn't tick all the boxes or is more than your preferred budget, but at that point is likely 'good enough' for the renters. I feel this is a kind of 'trap' agents use to ensure you take a less than ideal property. Should you feel the agent is showing you less than adequate properties, I would advise reaffirming with the agent clearly your requirements. Should these requirements not be met on the next viewing, find a new agent.

Making an offer

If the price seems too high, request a price drop. You can usually negotiate rent if you are willing to sign a longer term contract. Therefore, if you have a two-year school contract, it may be worthwhile signing for two years. However, being 'locked in' to a two-year contract with a penalty for breaking it, is the disadvantage.

Top tips

After you decide upon a property:

1. This may seem obvious, but as you view your dream home, do not show the realtor/landlord how keen you are. Unless you are moving to an area in which properties are in high demand, showing your undying love for a property will work against you if you wish to negotiate the rental price.
2. Ask for everything you would like to be included in the property and check the reliability of all items within the

apartment, such as lights, shower heads, beds, washer, fly nets, fridge, dishwasher, air con units, etc. This is possibly your only bargaining time. The landlord will be prepared to do the most to get you to move in and may do very little after the move, unless you have a major issue.

3. Check your contract thoroughly before signing. Ask what the landlord will cover should there be a burglary, water damage, typhoon, etc. Check whether electronic equipment is covered should it break. Request HR also check your contract to ensure it is fair and if written in dual language, the two translations match one another.

4. Insist on a full professional clean of the apartment and include white goods and air cons/heaters. Cleaning to this standard can be very expensive.

5. Question the agent/landlord about paying bills, parking space allocation, garbage collection, gas bottle delivery, and so on. This way there are no surprises when you move. Before you sign, you may wish to see previous bills to check what the overall cost of the bills may average.

6. Agree on how the rent will be paid, i.e. monthly or bi-monthly, via bank transfer or in cash, etc.

7. Ask to meet the landlord. This is important to establish a positive relationship with them, as you will often find they are more amenable once they know you and therefore may sort out problems and repairs more quickly.

Sort out the deposit and rent payments quickly. This will secure a good relationship with the landlord. Be aware that this could involve up to two months' deposit plus two months' rent, therefore have this cash available. Pay *only* a smaller deposit until all the work you have asked for has been carried out.

> I have always had a better experience renting a property after I have met the landlord. Once, when I requested a cheap washer (which was agreed), the landlord met my family and liked us so much he insisted on an upgraded washer! You are more likely to receive a quick response/better response to problems the better you know the landlord.

Banking

Your school should support you in setting up a local bank account. After that, you may well be on your own! Depending on the country, you may or may not have online banking. Ask the school about which branches most teachers use, as they may offer a basic level of English. This will be necessary as a bank transfer to your home country may need to be done manually, through the branch. It is a good idea to transfer money fairly regularly, every two or three months, back to a secure account in your home country. Ask your buddy or colleagues the best way to do this. Money sent back to the UK is likely to receive interest and there is also the security of understanding the banking system.

> Whilst in Egypt, frequently the banking system would be 'down' or cash machines wouldn't work. This and the stability of the country made me prefer to move cash out of the country as quickly as possible.

Safety and emergencies

Situations can change rapidly when living abroad, especially in less stable countries. Some examples which have affected international teachers include regional and national revolts, earthquakes, civil war, and pandemics.

As a priority, when you first move it is necessary to create a 'grab bag' for any situation in which you may need to leave quickly. This would include your passport, cash and credit cards, water and food plus any important documents you would struggle to replace. Keep copies of your most important documents in your home country, or another secure place outside of the country. Also recommended is purchasing a small safe for your home to keep your documents and valuables.

Furthermore, register with the home country embassy/representative office so that you get updates or get contacted in case of emergency/disaster.

When emergencies happen, it is important to have both contacts in the host country and at home that you can rely on. The most interesting outcome of such situations can be how a school reacts. If they are supportive and consider the wellbeing of their staff then this is a huge drawcard for new teachers to a school. As previously mentioned, it is worthwhile discussing the response of an international school to unprecedented events both with the leadership team and teachers. One teacher explained:

> *"When we gathered as a staff to discuss the matter, it was broken up angrily by the Head. After having nothing but positive experiences from this school, the situation shook me up a great deal and ensured I would not re-sign [a contract] with them. In a second situation, in a different international school, the management responded quickly and decisively to protect staff and students. This action made me have faith in the school management at that time."*

Remember, some situations are not what locals would consider an 'emergency'. Such examples include typhoons and earthquakes in countries in Asia. You may well be expected to continue teaching after a strong earthquake, as this is what local teachers may do.

Health

Through your school buddy, HR, or social media, inquire about reputable, English-speaking doctors and dentists to register with. There may be several options and it makes sense, before school starts, to visit them. It also is a good idea to locate the nearest hospital which has English-speaking staff. Discuss both with HR and/or colleagues about the best way to get to hospital in an emergency; in some countries a taxi is advised over an ambulance as they are more efficient.

Phone contract

After you have settled a little, ask around to see what other teachers use. You can also find out which local shops have the best English speakers to support you.

CHAPTER **5**

Settling in and Thriving

Following your arrival and securing an apartment, your next step is to adjust and settle. Here are some considerations at this stage.

Induction/social events

The process of moving can be disorientating and exhausting. You may experience culture shock and anxiety. Often when you first arrive, in addition to all the jobs you need to do such as sorting out a home, car, groceries, furniture, etc., there may be many non-obligatory social events.

To help you adjust and begin to feel settled, pinpoint which events you want to attend, ideally those which match your interests and preferences. Both learning about your new community and establishing yourself within it can really help combat initial culture shock. Should you have a family, focus on family events where other children will be present to help your child settle and to meet other parents.

During two of my moves, I endeavoured to attend every social event, even though I was tired and not at my best. During my third move, I could not attend all of the events, as I had a small child. However, when school started, I was able to meet people in small groups (which I prefer anyway), at my own pace.

But remember, if you need down time, your own wellbeing is the most important factor at this stage; friends can be made over time. Nevertheless, one teacher stressed that this was a period where she felt it was very important to attend every event:

> "…it's like a Fresher's Week at university; you need to attend everything to work out who will be your friends and who will remain just a colleague. It's really important to put yourself out there, or you may end up without friends in the early days."

Establishing a friendship group

When you first arrive, you may worry that you will not meet friends with similar interests. It's important to remember that you don't need to only be friends with fellow teachers; both expats and locals in the outside community can be fantastic for helping you integrate and feel settled.

In order to develop a social network, join clubs which interest you and establish friends outside of work. To find these clubs, contact your school buddy or post on local Facebook groups and other social media. While taking precautions to stay safe, you may also wish to post that you are new to the area and ask if anyone would like to meet up and show you around.

If you have children, seek out parent groups. That way you can socialise with others who have common interests and at the same time, the kids will be entertained.

Another great resource is 'InterNations', an expat organisation that is active in most countries. They often host networking events. These meetups are either free to join, or charge a small fee. They can easily be found with an internet search.

Some of my closest friends I have met outside of my workplace, just by being friendly and approaching them. I have met ladies in the gym, at the swimming pool, and at the hairdressers. Living abroad is different to home, as expats are often more open to conversation, as we are a minority. In every instance, I have found that striking up a conversation is very rewarding.

Missing loved ones

Homesickness is likely to affect you at some point after your move. One teacher described it thus:

> *"Wherever you go, it is human nature to compare it to where you have been before but this is not helpful. I began to miss the things I could only get in the UK and these became very special when I could find them in shops. Once I started to embrace the new things in the country, it really started to feel more like home."*

This can be a difficult period, therefore connect with your family and close friends quickly to help counteract this. Set up the internet within your apartment as soon as possible. As stressed previously, you can connect via a platform you like to use and can access in your new country, such as Skype or Facetime. Knowing that family and loved ones are a quick call away can be hugely reassuring. Video calling adds a further dimension, especially for children. However, be sure to research which social networks are available in a country prior to arrival, as some may not be available. Some countries ban particular sites.

Missing loved ones can be more challenging for children. My daughter only sees her Grandma once a year, but she has created a close bond, as Grandma reads with her twice a week and plays alongside her every Saturday morning. If you set up video calls, this is a simple way to maintain the bond.

Prioritising your own needs

If you have a fully-furnished apartment, add your own touches, even if it is just with small decorative items. Again, contact your buddy or support groups to find out the best places to purchase household items. Many schools set this up as part of their induction programme.

A great option is to find second-hand items through classifieds placed in Google+ groups, Facebook groups, or via staff who are selling their belongings. Make your apartment feel like home as quickly as you can.

Wellbeing

A very important aspect of a successful, happy life abroad is your own wellbeing. This section discusses how to improve your life within the host country and school. However, there are aspects of being an international teacher which you cannot control. This could be a national disaster, a pandemic, or a toxic, difficult school environment.

Having lived and worked through these uncontrollable events, I would argue that each situation is very personal to the individual going through it. Not everyone feels the same when faced with a similar situation.

If you do feel consistently unhappy and irritable or prone to tears or mood swings, it is vital that you seek professional help as soon as possible. Should you be unable to access help in-country, there are online mental health specialists, some of which are listed in Appendix B. If you feel comfortable, let others know what you are going through, such as your line manager, and ask for their support.

Getting involved in the school

When things settle down at school and you feel you have the time, ask yourself what could be done to improve the school, department, or your year group. It is important to remember that your experiences in other workplaces may have a valuable impact on the school you are currently in. Actively voice any ideas or improvements you can envision. However, be aware you may not always be heard initially, but do not be discouraged. Not only will opportunities to develop ideas support your own professional development, but they will make you feel more 'useful' or part of the running of the school.

In one school, I identified a need and approached SLT with my solution. I faced a panel to discuss this (which was scary). The idea was well-considered but could not practically take place. However, a second idea, which I raised later, was taken on board.

Further, get to know the staff and students well. A teacher explains how supporting the school, amongst other things, helped her settle:

"I settled by getting to know people, putting a lot of effort into adjusting in my new school, getting to know the families and the students really well, and taking the initiative to add elements from my previous schools into the delivery of lessons in my new school."

Getting involved in the community

Supporting the community in which you live can be hugely rewarding and it is a way you can make a difference. Consider doing some voluntary work and/or check whether the school runs any community support projects. If they do not, find established projects through your buddy, the school, or the wider community via social media. You will often find opportunities such as conservation initiatives, beach clean-ups, supporting at animal shelters, working in orphanages, or teaching English to local children.

You may also identify a potential need for a certain activity within your community, such as a specific sport. Connect with other teachers and the wider community to see if there is any interest, effectively widening your social sphere. If the activity is sport, contact the PE teachers to see if the school grounds and equipment could be used.

One teacher described how she met her 'community' outside of the school:

> *"I started volunteering in a local Greek school in Kuwait. I met people that became like family and who helped me have a taste of home here, too."*

Travel

Explore your local area and beyond, however, stay safe by asking others about common problems. Seek out activities which you cannot do in your own country; for example, visit a night market or tourist attraction, swim at the beach, or sample local cuisines. Research places of interest through a guide such as the 'Lonely Planet', through the Tripadvisor app, or even by checking Google maps for places of interest. A teacher explained how this supported her transition:

> *"[I] learned more of the language and travelled around the country first, rather than always travelling*

overseas. It was easier to then understand the country, people, and language."

If your host country is well-connected with airports, you can travel easily on your weekends and breaks. A tip for finding cheap destinations from your country is to use Skyscanner, either through the app or online. Enter your city in the 'from' box and for 'where to', try the 'anywhere' search box. This will list destinations from your city in order of price.

It is also worth approaching local travel agents. As agents buy tickets early and in bulk, they can often match or offer slightly cheaper prices than online. This works especially well when your salary is paid in local currency. You can pay by cash and therefore not use 'home' credit cards where the money can be subject to conversion rates and possible other charges. It is worth considering the ability to travel around – and out of – the country you move to.

Transport

If you are in a well-connected city, you may decide to only use public transport. Many cities now have easy-to-use and highly affordable bus and train routes. Using public transport can therefore save a lot of money and hassle in terms of maintaining a vehicle.

However, should you wish to explore more remote places easily, you may want to buy a vehicle. A great place to start is to ask other teachers whether they know of any colleagues selling their vehicles. However, if you want a newer vehicle or one with low mileage you can approach a dealership. If you have the option, it would be beneficial to have a speaker of the local language with you, and/ or someone who knows a little about vehicles. If you decide to buy, contact a mechanic to look over your prospective purchase. Also check the seller's contract thoroughly, which may need to be translated.

In terms of being able to drive, in some countries you will be able to swap your country's driving license, should there be a reciprocal licencing agreement in place. You can also use an UK-issued International Driving Permit in many countries. As these permits currently need to be renewed each year, you or someone you nominate will need to buy one for you from a UK post office. Wherever possible, it is advised that you learn to drive in your host country and sit the local driving test, so you can be fully aware of the rules.

I chose to buy a car whilst living in Taiwan. Personally, although we live in a well-connected city, I love the freedom and convenience of a car. This was not a cheap option; maintenance per year has cost around £1,500-2000. The car is maintained with a full service and regular maintenance at a professional garage. This gives me peace of mind, as when I travel, I know there is not a roadside assist available!

Pursuing other interests

If you have done your research well, you should know the expectations for how much time you will need to devote to your job and consequently how much free time you will have. In most instances, the work/life balance abroad should be better than at home.

Therefore, this is an opportune time to try recreational pursuits such as cycling, golf, climbing, amateur dramatics, or singing in a choir. There may also be additional opportunities to work, such as modelling, tutoring, or developing your own business. Should you be partaking in paid work, check if you are allowed to do this in your school contract and if there are any tax implications.

Furthermore, investigate what is currently 'missing' from your host country and you may see other opportunities. For example, there are teachers who have gone into comedy, opened restaurants, and even set up their own kindergarten.

 During my time in Vietnam raising my daughter, I ran my own pre-school business. I identified a venue through word-of-mouth and contacts and established the business, initially with friends as clients. I then promoted myself through Facebook groups and advertising. The business became popular and successful. I thoroughly enjoyed this experience as my first taste at running a business.

Finance

This may have been an important factor in relocating to teach abroad. Packages which include housing, healthcare, flights, and a good (often tax free) salary can be very appealing. There is a huge temptation to live an extravagant lifestyle and travel to expensive, luxurious destinations.

However, when you start international teaching, or at the first point you can save, you should. The longer you save, the sooner you will have accrued enough to retire. Being an international teacher will, most likely, mean that you will not have any kind of retirement plan as part of your work (although there are some schools which do offer this). Therefore, you need to think about how you will fund the 30+ years you are likely to need to support yourself through retirement. One director explains:

> *"It is so important to understand pensions and property buying in your home country. The longer you are abroad, the more difficult these become."*

How to save for retirement

Many people save through 'high interest' accounts, which can be based in your home country or offshore. In recent years, these accounts have offered ever-decreasing interest rates, with the majority now offering less than one percent and are subject to tax. Even ISAs, which offer tax-free savings, still have low rates. If you live abroad, you are not permitted to add to your ISAs. Therefore, saving in this way is unlikely to accrue enough money, in real terms (plus inflation), for retirement.

International teachers therefore need to consider how to fund their retirement. Teachers generally use two options: buy a property or invest. To support your financial decisions, it is well worth talking to a financial advisor before you depart your host country.

When I first began teaching internationally, I had something booked every single holiday, usually in another country. As a teaching couple, we saved very little. We began to cut back after transferring to one salary, so saved even less. Now, returning to combined salaries, we have been able to save. I wish we had started earlier.

Purchasing property

It is difficult, if not impossible, to get a mortgage when living abroad. However, some teachers maintain a property they bought when living in the UK or buy a property outright when abroad. This can be quite an attractive prospect as, after the property is purchased, it can be rented out and therefore the mortgage can be paid whilst you live abroad. There are difficulties with this, however. Many teachers have explained that less-than-desirable tenants, or constant issues with the property, have caused stress and difficulties which are challenging to deal with when abroad. There is also a tax implication, as renting out a property becomes taxable income. Buy-to-let/rent properties are very difficult to obtain a mortgage for.

A solution to rental issues is hiring an agent to take care of your property. Agents can act as an intermediary between yourself and the tenants. They can help arrange workers to complete necessary upkeep and also vet possible tenants for your property. If you do go down this route, it is highly recommended that you research the agent well and ensure they have many recommendations from clients, preferably people you know of. There are unfortunately cases of agents not upholding their role and therefore tenants becoming very unsatisfied if they cannot have their issues dealt with. Yet, one colleague did not find the use of an agent necessary, as she explains:

> *"[My husband and I] have managed our own houses, one for 11 years and one for 2 years, since we bought them. We used an agent for the initial check and contract then just did it all ourselves."*

Investing

The other route for saving for retirement, is investment. In order to understand the basics of investing, it is recommended you read Andrew Hallam's 'Millionaire Expat'. Within this book, he details why you should invest independently of financial advisors. He argues that financial advisors always charge a fee, taking a percentage of your interest through their own charges (169). He believes they are no more able to predict or 'beat' stock markets than anyone else (46). Instead, he recommends you contribute to a brokerage directly. You can try to do this yourself with the guidance of the book. Or, if you'd like support, you can contact PlanVision, owned by Mark Zoril and recommended by Hallam. PlanVision provide detailed videos, as well as online support to set up a brokerage. Alternatively, should you have the time and means, above all, consider contacting a financial advisor for full advice.

I began investing at the start of the COVID-19 stock market decline with the advice of Mark Zoril. I had no idea of the process and his videos and support guided me through what to expect. Initially I appeared to lose a large percentage of what I invested. But over the course of two months, I had regained the difference plus interest.

Subsequent relocations

There are likely multiple reasons why you may decide to move on from your school. You may consider the living environment no longer suitable, you want to advance to a different role, the work environment may have become less desirable, or perhaps you just fancy a change.

When seeking a new position, you are at a distinct advantage. Due to your initial experience, you will know what you are looking for (or perhaps avoiding) and your international experience will generally work in your favour. Therefore, your search can be streamlined to the countries and schools which you know will suit you. Furthermore, when you interview or apply to an agency, it will not be a new process. Remember to use your contacts too; ask colleagues where they enjoyed working, or for any contacts they have who currently enjoy their workplace. Word-of-mouth can also be useful in finding out about new positions within schools. In addition, if a Headteacher you have really enjoyed working with is moving on, you can see if you can 'follow' them to their new school.

If you decide to contact schools directly, again it is wise to sell yourself in the cover letter, read their mission statement, and look through their website. Explain why the school needs you, referring to – and emphasising – your current international experience and how your experience can support their ethos. Should you decide to visit a top choice school, which is highly advisable, you know what to look out for. During the visit, comment on similarities/

differences with your current international school and projects you could bring to the school. Praise all the good things you see in the school. If it transpires that the school has a high percentage of EAL children, mention how you support them within your current class and any training or qualifications you have in this area. Remember that with second and subsequent moves, you have more to sell about yourself, so don't miss opportunities to do this!

However, be mindful that leaving a posting may be more difficult than you envisage in terms of breaking away from your expat community.

One surprising factor which crept up on me was leaving friends. I could not see all the positives in my new posting, as the colleagues I met there did not match up to my old community. My advice would be to take each move as a new adventure. If possible, move somewhere very different to your last, so that comparisons are more difficult to make.

Breaking contract

Most schools require you to sign a two- or three-year contract. This can be daunting, as it is not uncommon that schools which on paper look ideal, in reality, are not. After the move, you may decide it is not a place you wish to work and/or a country in which you wish to live. The working environment may not be a positive one for you. At this point it is important you speak to someone within the Senior Leadership Team to see if they can support you in any way. If you are honest and have genuine reasons for leaving the school, there could well be an 'amicable' breakup.

It is worth noting that breaking contract could affect subsequent job offers. I would only advise breaking contract after a short time if you have a very good reason to do so. Breaking contract without a strong, 'valid' reason is always something which would be questioned and you would likely be viewed as a flight risk. One Senior Leader within a school warned:

> *"I think it's hard to leave a gap on your CV. When I look at CVs, it concerns me if there is a gap so I would maybe suggest something like adding a comment below the dates to say, left prior to end of contract due to personal reasons."*

Although I have never broken contract, I have had colleagues that have needed to do this. One case was due to the many difficulties one friend encountered within the country and subsequent difficulties at the school. Thankfully, she appealed to the management and, due to her mental health, was not penalised for breaking contract.

CHAPTER 6

International Teacher Types and Dependents

A single teacher abroad

M aking the move independently will present both advantages and challenges.

An advantage is that you will not need to agree or negotiate your choice of destination and/or school with anyone else. You can consider the countries and schools in which you personally will thrive. In addition, if you do not have a partner or any dependents, you are less costly for the school to hire, as they will only be providing benefits for you. So, in theory, you should have the pick of more schools.

The disadvantages of moving alone can include the lack of immediate support from a partner when you first arrive. Even considering the best induction support, when you initially move you are likely to feel disorientated, and having someone sharing those experiences with you can help. To counteract this, immediately contact your school 'buddy' and others you will have networked with before the move. It is therefore important to know whether you will be entering into a friendly environment; even more so if you are travelling alone. One single teacher explained:

> *"The staff at my first school were very warm and welcoming and that really helped. I was also very lucky and met a lot of wonderful people who helped me settle really quickly."*

Furthermore, you won't have another person to share the initial jobs with (house hunting, buying furniture, etc.) or to discuss decisions with. If your school organises few social events or activities, you may also struggle. Again, this is something to ask current staff about. Find out what clubs or activities are currently running for teachers and join up. For example, international school teachers often join sports clubs, books clubs, and dining clubs.

Another challenge will be if you start working at a school with only one or two new staff, as this may limit your choice of friends. Depending on the school, there may be long-term staff who are less likely to break up their friendship groups, or invite you in. Look carefully at the demographics of the school. As a single teacher, you may well be able to create a support network quickly if there are teachers of a similar demographic as you. However, if the majority of staff have families, you may not find you 'fit' in these social groups as easily, unless you love children outside of work too of course.

If you are seeking a romantic attachment, again check the demographics of the school, as well as the experiences of other expats within your chosen country. If you choose to have a relationship with an expat, or local, there may be attitude and cultural differences to consider. One single female teacher explains:

> *"[Meeting a partner was] not as easy for me, as there were mainly couples in both schools I worked at and it isn't as easy in Kuwait to meet single people."*

Conversely, one single male teacher said:

> *"Particularly for men it is easier, but it all depends on the place and culture."*

Overall, single teachers felt the cultural and language difference could be a barrier and in fact made it difficult to connect with others romantically. Further, relationships with colleagues were often difficult, not only because you work with them, but also because schools often employ teaching couples. One single teacher said:

> *"I found that good old fashioned Tinder and a lot of patience worked. I also found a local man who had lived abroad for some of his life too, which helped us to have more in common. Another good way to [meet others] is to join groups outside of your workplace in things like art clubs, hiking etc."*

Teaching couples

An obvious advantage for the school for taking on a teaching couple is the ability to save in terms of the contract benefits. The cost of combining housing for teaching couples is often cheaper than paying two single allowances, for example. However, the larger joint housing benefit is advantageous for the teaching couple, as this allows for bigger, 'better' apartment rentals.

Moving as a teaching couple offers an element of stability. You have equal opportunities to partake in work and, if you are on the same point on the pay scale, you will have the benefit of receiving double the salary. Entering a new situation with someone by your side and sharing the same experiences can support teachers, especially in the early stages of transition. When you get home after work, you are able to talk everything over with someone you trust.

The shared holiday breaks allow travel opportunities together and you have the time to explore your new destination. Tasks and responsibilities in your personal life can be shared, such as shopping and filling in documentation. Sharing these roles, especially when simple errands can be quite stressful, will help a great deal initially. One teacher explained:

> *"You are in it together and understand the feelings the other has, especially at the beginning. Your partner can help answer questions you might have about the school and vice versa. You experience all the highs and lows together. I wouldn't have been brave enough to come to Taiwan if I was not part of a teaching couple."*

Both within and outside of school, you create different networks due to where you teach in the school and your hobbies. Therefore, you can make lots of friends to share with each other.

However, there are challenges. Some teachers who move abroad when young may never have experienced living with a partner before. This new experience, in addition to the extra time spent together in both home and school (dependent on whether you are both in the same school or on the same campus), can strain some couples. Coming home and discussing work can also lead to a situation where work becomes central to a couple's lives. Furthermore, if one person is unhappy with their situation, there is pressure on the other regarding whether to resign or not. One partner may not have their contract renewed whilst the other is offered a further contract. Additionally, some countries are not accepting of same-sex couples or living with a boyfriend or girlfriend. Check these limitations carefully should these affect you.

Furthermore, it may not be possible to both secure jobs in your most desirable school/location at the same time. Should this happen, one teacher explained that:

> *"Patience is key; if you find the right place, it is sometimes worth taking that leap of faith with only one job and finding your feet when you get there. Often opportunities come up for the trailing spouse further down the line."*

Raising a family abroad

Many teachers begin their international career not considering this eventuality. Other teachers already have children who will accompany them on the move.

If you are a long-term expat teacher already, there is a lot to consider when thinking about having children abroad. One or two children are often given free school places. However, more than two are often considered too costly for a school. Therefore, you may have to pay all, or a part of, the fees yourself.

It is also important to think carefully about the relative impact having children will have on your expat life. One international teacher explained:

> *"...if your expat life revolves around experiences, such as restaurants, socialising, trips, etc., you may struggle with this change. It is very rare to be able to be 'gung ho' and go for it; everything needs to be planned. This depends on the individual of course. Further, travel can be limited, due to worries about the food options and healthcare in other countries."*

For those who start a family whilst abroad, review whether your school's health insurance includes care during pregnancy and covers costs for births. Investigate these benefits, including maternity/

paternity leave, and research the quality of hospitals in the country. Leading up to the birth, you may be happy with the level of care provided in the country, or you may prefer to give birth in your home country surrounded by family. This is entirely a personal decision.

Research your hospital well by gaining advice and recommendations from both locals and expats. Private international hospitals or clinics do not always equal the best in terms of provision or value for money. The advantage of giving birth in the country you have relocated to is that you will be settled in your own home and able to use a hospital in which you will have had regular visits. In some countries, you may even have the option of choosing your doctor for delivery. Depending on your insurance cover, the premium can include having your baby delivered privately, often in your own room. One teacher stated:

> *"Having a child abroad was so easy. The school paid for all the expenses of the birth through the Bupa insurance. It was a lovely experience and I had a private room and lots of options. The doctors all spoke English."*

Many teachers have used a doula during the birthing process, often one who is also fluent in the local language. These ladies will guide and support you through childbirth, in addition to mediating between yourself and the hospital staff. If you have previously given birth, teachers have recommended that you bring your previous birth notes so that you can share them with your consultant. This may help with both the delivery and post-birth aftercare.

A disadvantage of having your child abroad is giving birth in a different culture to yours, where perhaps certain procedures may be more readily applied (such as caesarean). Even at the check-up visits, there may be miscommunication due to language or a lack of understanding of vaccinations given in the country of your birth. When in hospital, in certain countries it will be difficult to communicate with anyone other than the doctor, unless you have an interpreter. In addition, you will not have the initial support of wider family and the system of aftercare (such as midwives) can be quite different to the UK. Therefore, it is very important that you consider these aspects. On a positive note, following birth in some countries (in particular Asia) you can stay in a 'post birth hotel', where you can have support to look after your baby. Your expectations of your birthing plan may need to adjust, however, as one teacher described:

> *"There is a marked contrast between the acceptance of midwife-led care and home birth in the UK and the generally more medicalised consultant-led care here in Taiwan. You definitely have to do your research here, to find a doctor/clinic that matches up with your preferences."*

Furthermore, it is extremely important you check the passport requirements. For example, in Vietnam, the process of securing a British passport for a child born of British parents is a lengthy, bureaucratic ordeal which can last up to one year. An international teacher explained that there can even be issues further in the future for your child if you give birth abroad:

> *"My child would need to have their child in the UK for the child to become a British Citizen as you can only pass British descent through one generation."*

Most international schools will clearly stipulate on their contracts if you are entitled to maternity/paternity leave. Schools vary in their provision for this leave. Some schools remunerate for a certain number of weeks, whilst others will grant leave but it will be unpaid. If leave is provided, you have the further consideration of whether you or your partner will stay at home to raise your child and for how long.

Some expats choose to stay at home in their host country, often with a nanny or home help. With the absence of family support, this can be a huge advantage. Often, the lower salaries for home help abroad can make hiring far more affordable than in the UK. Often teachers have returned to work and taken on a full-time nanny, either live-in or out. If you decide on this option, there is the concern of who to trust. Research your nanny well and preferably recruit a nanny who has come recommended with references and is happy to complete a police check. Also check legal hiring procedures and contract expectations, including visas and benefits, flights, and holiday pay. There are multiple groups on Facebook and social media platforms in most areas of the world specifically for seeking nannies; you can either search for these directly, or enquire on the 'ladies' groups or expat groups in the area you move to. One international teacher described home help with her children as a huge advantage:

> *"Being able to afford extra help at home and a better standard of living is a real plus. In the UK, we really struggled to make ends meet on our combined teaching salaries, now we are able to save and still have a good quality of life."*

As having a child can be a huge adjustment, it is a good idea to establish a community of parents whom you can spend time with in the day to help you and your child socialise. Join a baby group/class as part of your expat experience. Some countries may not have these established. If this is the case, set up your own! One expat mother explained:

> *"The lack of familial support is a huge disadvantage. I am lucky because I have made strong and meaningful friendships, so I had wonderful emotional support. This is rare, however, and I see many expat mothers struggle being so far away from family."*

It can be difficult, or impossible, to find certain products you want for your child. Examples include specific medicines, nappy cream, or even certain brands of nappies. Certain toys can be very expensive or unavailable. If there is anything you feel you will need, try to ship them prior to the birth, through contacts in your home country if possible, or through providers such as Amazon.com.

Finally, decide the vaccination schedule you will follow. You may opt to follow the schedule of the country in which you live, especially if you are planning to stay for an extended period, or you can follow your home country's schedule. Check what you need via websites such as the NHS for the UK. Be aware that some vaccination requirements of your host country may differ to those recommended in the UK, due to the prevalence of certain diseases.

When I knew I was pregnant, I immediately reached out to the community. I first set up a pregnancy support group which grew to a baby group where we took turns to visit each other's houses for playdates. The children grew up together and we began toddler meetups in play centres. To do this, I simply posted on a Facebook group in the local area to generate interest. The group started quite small and mainly attracted expats, but by the time I was posting for the toddler group, it had expanded to become more diverse.

Dependent children

If your child is very young, research options for day-care and the relevant costs. It is important to check that the hours day-care can offer allow you time to be in school, as well as in after-school meetings. An advantage of international schools is that if your children are of school age, they should be able to attend your international school for a reduced cost or for free. This can be appealing as, if you have chosen your school carefully, it should provide your child with an excellent education.

In many schools, the facilities and resources are state of the art, and may include swimming pools, gyms, STEM centres, and 1:1 device availability. There are usually specialist teachers and departments. Further, opportunities for after-school activities, such as dance, music, and sports in particular, are abundant in most international schools. Children will have the opportunity to experience a completely different lifestyle and culture to the one they had at home. They can benefit from multi-cultural experiences and have friends from all over the world. Furthermore, their teacher parent(s) achieving a work/life balance often translates to a happier family environment. Travelling to and from the school together is far less stressful than trying to arrange pick up and drop off. One teacher parent explained the advantages for them were:

"...giving our children the experience of living in another culture and also of them gaining places in good schools with many opportunities for them."

However, check the school provisions for your child's age or year group. In some schools, the secondary departments are not so well established or resourced as the primary, and vice versa. Furthermore, if your child/ren have any special needs or requirements, check that these can be accommodated at the school and/or within the wider community (if specialist support is required). If this support is available at the school or within the community, check if there are any fees as this can be expensive. However, many international schools do not have provision for Special Educational Needs and you may not be able to find the specialised help you need within the community.

Some teachers opt to have their child/ren educated outside of their school, in the local language. This can be quite an advantage if you would like your child to learn the native language, or you prefer the provision elsewhere. Ensure you research the educational systems available, as it is likely there will be several to choose from. Be aware that often parents in other countries have different expectations of their children, which may not match yours. Therefore, whichever educational institution you choose, be sure to check the school's ethos in terms of academics and wellbeing, to ensure the expectations are in line with your own.

There is an element of concern that your child's native language may be affected. For example, living in a society where English is not spoken will reduce their opportunities to share conversations with others and hear their language in the environment. One international teacher commented:

> "I am worried my daughter's spoken language ability is slipping. When we used to travel back to the UK every six months, she picked up a lot of language there, but nowadays we cannot. I don't think her language has moved on significantly in the past year or so."

Nevertheless if, within this new environment, your children are able to embrace learning the local language, this can be an excellent skill for their future. This is particularly the case if you are based in a country with a widely spoken language, such as French, Spanish or Mandarin. Having a broader understanding of the world can help develop your child into a true global citizen. They will become more resilient, having had to navigate life in a different culture and language.

The society may offer a safer environment with less crime and drug issues than the country you have relocated from. Dependent on both the culture and the school, there can be far fewer cases of bullying in countries outside the UK. This is especially relevant if you are moving abroad with older children. Thoroughly research the country and school to ensure there are opportunities for your children to enjoy life and thrive in the host country. However, be aware that, for older children, there will likely be fewer opportunities in terms of part-time jobs. In addition, if English is not the most commonly spoken language within school, they may experience frustration due to the language barrier. Often this limits their friendships to those children they are able to communicate with.

Should your child be of school age, this can be a great way to settle in – by connecting with other teachers and parents with school-aged children. One trailing spouse explained:

> *"[The] children's school really helped me to settle. It established a routine for us, and provided connections to other families/friends."*

Investigate the best neighbourhoods to live for families, such as family-friendly apartments or compounds. If travel is important to you, ensure the neighbourhood is well connected with transport and there are places to visit which interest you all. This is a great opportunity for children to see more of the world. Be mindful that the requirements for young children and teenagers, both in terms of neighbourhoods and at school, can differ wildly. Younger children will need outside space and parks, whilst teenagers may prefer malls and entertainment. One international teacher particularly recommends Taiwan with young children, as:

> *"...it is very child-friendly here; lots of great free play centres and parks on every corner; lots of things to do for children of all ages."*

If you choose your country and school carefully, you can ensure the ethos is one which matches what you truly want for your children. With your buddy, talk through whether there are community events and groups that teachers' children can be a part of, which can help children to settle. Establishing a friendship base prior to the move for your children, through requesting playdates, can really help them to settle quickly. Expats and teachers often report this can be the most challenging aspects of the move. Taking the children away from their extended family can be a real struggle. One trailing spouse explained that the change for her child was challenging:

"My then seven-year-old enjoyed her life back home and was reluctant to move. After the move, she definitely felt alienated and lonely because she couldn't speak the language and had no friends. Hence, a British school has been great for her/us. I was also ridden with guilt for taking [the children] away from what they loved, and my not understanding that when they were behaving badly/abnormally it was because they didn't feel settled."

It is very important you research the healthcare system and hospitals thoroughly, especially in terms of providing healthcare for children. For example, establish whether or not there are international/English-speaking paediatricians and hospitals. If you do find an English-speaking paediatrician, you need to check that they understand your ideas and priorities too. When you move to the country, find the locations of health clinics and doctors quickly and register. Experiencing an emergency situation in a different country can be terrifying, especially when the systems are different and language is a barrier. One international teacher explained:

"Rushing at 11pm to A and E when we had only been in the country a couple of months was terrifying. They would not accept our child, who was struggling to breathe, until we located her health card and they checked it. Then we had to sit and wait. Thankfully, although language was a huge barrier, she was put on a respirator relatively quickly."

Pollution and quality of life is also is a big consideration when moving abroad with children. Some countries, such as China, have very high levels of pollution in certain cities. However, often these countries do have air purifiers within schools and you can purchase them for your home. When levels of pollution reach a certain level, children stay inside the school. Some schools provide purpose built indoor areas such as pollution controlled play and sports facilities.

A disadvantage of moving with children is that family, in most cases, will not join you. It can therefore be difficult for children to maintain their links to home and they can feel disconnected from their home culture. For parents, living without an extended support network can be a strain. That is where a paid helper may be able to support you. Often helpers can also cook, clean, babysit and run the house. This can afford you more quality time with your children. One teacher recommends that, in order to sustain the wellbeing of your children, it is important to:

> *"Maintain family and cultural links as much as possible; ensure that their bedrooms are personal and are a priority to set up when you move."*

Expats and teachers state that they feel that friendships are easier to make abroad as parents. This is due to more parents having similar experiences and lifestyles. The flip side of this, though, is the transient nature of living abroad. There is a constant movement of people, in or out of the country. This can be difficult as a parent, yet is even more so for a child. One trailing spouse explained that she witnessed her son struggle:

> *"...losing close friends often [is hard] – one year, my son lost his entire 'gang' of friends at the same time."*

In many, if not all, countries, your child will be considered foreign or an outsider by locals. This can at times be an advantage, affording them positive attention. But as your child grows, they may feel this displacement and no longer enjoy such attention. Children who grow up as expats are often known as 'third culture children' and there has been a lot of research on the displacement these children can feel (for article and text references, see Appendix C). As a family, you should be clear on what you are all looking for in the move. It helps to talk through the realities of the move clearly and in as much detail as possible.

Trailing spouse/partner

It is essential that you also consider how your partner might be able to work, create their own community, and pursue their interests within the host country, whilst you are at work. It is important that your spouse or partner remains happy. Before moving abroad, research job opportunities in addition to work permits for a partner should they wish to work at some point. This may be not at the time of the move, but perhaps within a few years. Their desire to work may change, especially if they have children who are at school all day. It is important to know this can be a possibility. Partners need to decide whether they are willing to stay home all day or, in most cases, take a job in a field other than their own (often working in the spouse's school).

In some countries, partners are able to work. However, a 'dependents' visa (which your school will usually procure for your partner and children) may not permit this. Places that do not offer work opportunities to partners are problematic. Many partners enjoy the freedom of being unemployed initially, but then begin to miss their careers, ability to meet adults, or earning their own income. Another option is to explore online and remote options for employment. This may well have tax implications, so you would need to also check this with HR, an accountant, or a financial adviser. One trailing spouse explained that she feels:

> "...insecure about not having my own work/income, but [I] feel privileged at the same time that I don't have to work simply for an income, but can take time to think about what I would really like to do, whether it's in the same field or not."

If your partner stays at home, it is a good idea to find expat groups and actively seek opportunities to make friends with local residents also. It can be an opportunity to pursue a hobby or develop a new one. To keep busy and to connect within the new society, seek out opportunities such as volunteering.

If the trailing partner does not work, it is important to be clear on expectations for one another. If one person is the sole wage earner, this could breed resentment or expectations for some couples. Yet not in all cases; one trailing spouse explained how considerate of this her husband was:

> *"My partner gave me a credit card. And he ALWAYS says, we've earned so much money this month (it varies). He still corrects me when I say, 'You earned X much'."*

However, it is important to clearly define roles. If one partner ends up being the home-maker all the time, this can be a negative position to be in if this is not what they had envisioned. One spouse shared:

> *"He doesn't help, ever, with the housework. I sometimes feel like a maid. But I know where he's coming from [as the wage earner], and I try to deal with it and not let it bother me."*

Being a teacher parent

A further consideration, and for some teachers perhaps the most difficult, is that often within international schools, you work with your child/ren who also attend the school. This can be challenging in that you have a double role: your child sees you as their parent and the school and students view you as a teacher. The two can cross over and you may need to stipulate the roles both to your child and to staff. Early on, if this is something important to you, ask your child's teacher to connect with you as a parent only in the defined parent meetings and not give out pieces of information that you would not otherwise receive.

In addition, it can be a struggle to be on the side-lines looking into your child's education through such a close lens. You will know the temperament and capabilities of their teacher, which is a challenge if they do not match your own. Yet, the plus side is that you often have front row seating at their school events and you do have insights into the curriculum they are being taught.

Initially, I struggled with the parent/teacher role, especially when my daughter was in Reception, as I felt she was so young. I caught myself watching her from the side-lines at times. I remember one time when she walked up to me in the middle of a PE lesson and I had to send her away. It was heart-breaking.

Managing early school starts and after school meetings, can be challenging if you have young children, unless you hire help. Alternatively, if possible, arrange for an after-school activity (within school) during this time, or ask what other teacher parents do. You may be able to take turns 'babysitting' after school for each other's children.

Further, as a teacher in the school, the position can feel different to other parents. Feeling that your child always has to appear 'as good as possible' in front of parents and other teachers can be really challenging. Also, you may not wish to socialise with parents, as inevitably some parent's children and siblings will overlap with children you teach. You may feel you cannot relax, or parents can at times feel the need to question you about their child or about school politics.

CHAPTER 7

Expat Voices

Captured below are the voices of both teachers and their trailing spouses. They show how overall, the experience of relocating abroad was a very positive one.

Why did you want to teach abroad?

The idea of a better work-life balance. Teaching for the children's needs rather than for Ofsted, as well as the chance to experience life elsewhere and meet new people, sounded very appealing. One of the people I spoke to had lived in Kuala Lumpur and the lifestyle sounded exactly like what I was after and, having been there before, I set my heart on going there. *Gemma, international teacher*

I moved to Cambodia because I wanted to travel and experience more in life before I settled down and found a partner and a home. I was very interested in Asia, having been there on holiday and whilst travelling, and thought it would be an exciting place to be. *Jo, international teacher*

We decided that our 30's should be spent having adventures and not living the life of a retired couple in Cornwall. My husband is a secondary teacher so we had the luxury of moving anywhere. *Trailing spouse*

I moved to Kuwait as I wanted to work overseas again and in order to help my family back home financially, mainly. *International teacher*

[We moved] first to Myanmar, for an adventure, culture, and a good [financial] package. *John, international teacher*

[It was a] way to travel and earn at the same time. *Kate, international teacher*

Teaching in England was becoming stressful and all about the paperwork and Ofsted. We wanted to get back to the actual important bit – teaching in the classroom. *Becky, international teacher*

It was a wonderful opportunity to learn more about teaching, and teach a wide range of ages and groups. *Jenny and Peter, international teaching couple*

What is important to consider for a move?

For us, healthcare and the education and fit of the school for our children are main priorities. We also wanted to live in a country that we felt comfortable with in terms of its politics and position on human rights, etc. *Kate, international teacher*

Safety is important to me. For us as a family, we have to ensure the country is stable and crime is low. We definitely worry more now that we have a child. [We wanted] a good quality of life, [and] now we live in Taiwan, I think how do we top this? *Keith, international teacher*

What were your first thoughts when you were offered the job?

I interviewed for a school in Kuala Lumpur and didn't get it, but was offered a job at their sister school in Yangon, Myanmar. My response (to myself and friends and family, not the school) was 'Yangon? Where is Yangon?' I researched it and spoke to others that lived there and decided to take a chance and go for it...[I'm] so glad I did as I'd say it's one of the best things I ever decided to do! *Gemma, international teacher*

When we got the job, we were elated and very excited; it felt like a new chapter in our lives and [an] amazing adventure. *Becky, international teacher*

When we first discussed it, I was so uncertain. While the idea was thrilling, the reality was terrifying. But the idea of doing something for us won us over; of being free of the ties of mortgages etc., and instead enjoy travel and work experiences we couldn't get from two week holidays each year. *Adele and Danny, teaching couple*

How did you feel, initially?

Pure excitement! *Trailing spouse*

Initially I had a mixture of excitement and nerves. I was anxious about lots of things, thinking 'will I make friends?', 'will I like the school?', 'will I like the place?', 'will I miss home?' Despite these nerves, I embraced the experience and have honestly loved every minute of it (if I ignore the impact of Covid and a military coup!) Straight away I felt that I had a home away from home. Everyone was so welcoming and helped me to settle. *Gemma, international teacher*

Wonderful! I loved everything about my first move abroad. Everything was new, exciting, and I found as a foreigner in Japan, it was very easy to meet people in a sociable and professional environment. *Michael, director of a kindergarten and early primary*

Terrified! I had never really thought about going to Vietnam, much less living there. I was nervous about how I would fit in and if people would be friendly. *Lucinda, trailing spouse*

[The] first night is always hard, I always wonder what on earth we are doing, and then things settle down, and you get into the swing of things. It can be overwhelming at the beginning; a lot to take in, new smells, new processes. It takes a while to take it all in. Sometimes school don't allow you enough time to settle in and it can be very overwhelming. *Jennie and Peter, international teaching couple*

Excited! And my school were really good at providing welcome packages and a fun initiation week before work started to get to know the country and to buy essentials. I only came over with two suitcases! *Esther, international teacher*

When we were on the plane, and for the first few days of being here, we questioned our decision to move; leaving family behind was very difficult and we were overwhelmed with how alien we felt when we got here. Within a couple of weeks those feelings faded and we were really pleased we moved here. *Becky, international teacher*

What made the transition easier? Were there struggles?

It usually takes us about six months to settle. For me, making friends always helps and I have to use all of my courage to invite some colleagues to go out socially. Every time I have done so, people have jumped at the opportunity, which always makes me wish I had done it sooner! *Clare, assistant principal*

It was hard arriving by myself and meeting everyone new, but attending all the socials in the first month helped me to meet as many people as I could to decide who I would fit in best with. It helped me form a small group of people who enjoyed the same things I did. *Esther, international teacher*

In our first week in Vietnam, we went out to a local restaurant with some other new teachers. We managed to order a whole chicken; boiled whole and chopped up, organs and all! Not a great culinary start but a great bonding experience. *Keith, international teacher*

Learning the basics of the language makes it easier; making new friends both at school and if possible, outside of the school; keeping your interests, hobbies, or sports going if possible; finding the good (everywhere has challenges, make the most of the time you have there). *John, international teacher*

Meeting our buddies was a turning point and made me realise it would all be ok. They answered all our questions and made us feel at ease. Moving into our apartment and getting on with exploring Taipei also helped. *Becky, international teacher*

Learning the basics of how a country functions is very helpful. You will feel more settled as soon as you know how things work. *Trailing spouse*

I started looking beyond the family, looking for connections/friendships. I felt a bit lonely at that time, as so much attention was given to how [the] husband is with his job and how [the] children are [at] school. As a trailing spouse, when the 'home' is settled, it's easy to feel that one's done one's job, when in reality that's not really one's sole purpose. *Trailing spouse*

How did you settle?

Relatively smoothly in all countries. The hardest part was living in an area with very few local shops. So, where you live is extremely important for a happier and easier time. *Michael, a director of a kindergarten and early primary*

About two thirds of the way through the school year, I think you begin to feel part of the furniture. Everyday things that on arrival would take more thought or adjusting to just become more comfortable. Before you realise it, you know where to go, or who to ask and you feel more relaxed in general. Get to know other families, spend time with them, make the effort to join social events and activities as much as possible. *Kate, international teacher*

We loved everything about each place we went and always did the same things to settle. We would meet as many of the teaching staff as possible and do all drinks/meetings/arranged activities in the first week or two, to make as many connections as possible. We also spent the first few days walking to new areas, heading in different directions, with no real agenda other than mapping the area in our brain. *Danny and Adele, teaching couple*

It's good to see some of the tourist sites in the first year and not just concentrate on work so you get a good feel of the country and you have memorable moments to think about when you begin to miss home. *Esther, international teacher*

I had found friends, established a pattern/rhythm in life, and could make plans for the future of where I wanted to go and explore. I settled well and had routine in my life/day which helped. *Jo, international teacher*

Having parent/women's groups to join and large expat communities definitely help. These become your support network when you don't have your family around and allow you to meet people in similar situations and make friends easily. These friendships can often be stronger or more meaningful than friendships back home, probably due to the levels of support they offer. *Trailing spouse*

We tried to eat in local rather than western restaurants to embrace the culture. Small things like working out how to get an online delivery made a big difference. And finding ingredients to cook our favourite dishes from home. When our shipping arrived, it made our apartment feel much more like home. *Becky, international teacher*

Good friends, good times, and a positive outlook. Being an excitable person helps, because even small tasks like paying bills in a new country is somewhat of an adventure. *Trailing spouse*

Have you done anything you are proud of?

[I'm] very proud of being able to work with people from different countries [and] cultures. [I am also] proud that I could travel to many different places and experience so many places and cultures. *Michael, director of a kindergarten and early primary*

I'm proud of having challenged myself to begin [teaching] a new subject whilst working abroad. Although I had had experience in my degree in Drama, I had not taught it. Being made Head of Department in a new school meant I was able to design my own curriculum and I enjoy the variety it now brings to my teaching. *Esther, international teacher*

I hope that I have made a positive change in the schools in which I work. *Clare, assistant principal*

I volunteered at an orphanage two evenings a week, as I found that I had spare time and I wanted to do something useful with this time. This was very rewarding and doing something that was impossible in the UK made me feel very positive about having moved aboard. *Jo, international teacher*

Vietnam was the best thing we have ever done. I'm proud I made lifetime girlfriends that are my sisters. We got to travel and save a lot of money. It was amazing. I would recommend this to anyone even considering it. *Lucinda, trailing spouse*

I am proud that a girl who doesn't really like change, who likes familiarity and regularity, ever did anything so crazy as to live and work abroad! I loved almost every minute of it, don't regret anything and am so thrilled that we chose to do such amazing things. Definitely an amazing experience. *Adele, teacher*

Would you do it again?

Yes, without hesitation. *Michael, director of a kindergarten and early primary*

Yes! I am off to Taiwan in July. *Gemma, international teacher*

Yes, I would. It has been an incredible experience working here and I have learnt and gained so much over the past seven years. *International teacher*

This is our second international position. We always planned to return to the UK, but the longer we are away, the harder I think it becomes to imagine picking up life back there. It would need to be a really special school, opportunity, or home, I think, to entice us back. *Kate, international teacher*

I would and I did! Once I married and had a child, we moved back to Asia together, which was fantastic and also a very different experience. *Jo, international teacher*

Absolutely! Once the world recovers and we can travel again without too many restrictions and [our] baby has met her family and grown a bit, we will be back – somewhere different, a new adventure. *John, international teacher*

In a heartbeat! In my 21 years as a teacher, I have spent 18 working away from my home country in four different countries and wouldn't change any of it! Now that my children are teenagers, we will be staying put for a while in Singapore, but I am excited to see what the future holds for my husband and I! *Clare, assistant principal*

What advice would you give to those teachers who are moving abroad for the first time?

If you don't have children, be brave, go crazy, and go somewhere you have never thought about or heard of. It's two years; you will grow and learn and have a blast if you are open. If you have a kid or two, you might need to think more carefully about health (e.g. Myanmar had very poor [healthcare] and we had to go to Bangkok), roads, cars, etc. I feel if you are willing to jump in and go with the flow, you will make it work and have a great time. *John, international teacher*

Be open to connect with the people and the culture of your new country. Learn the culture of the school and engage with your department in order to bond with your colleagues. *Isabelle, expat coach*

Find your own tribe; take risks and reach out to others. Accept that moving to, and settling in, a new place will be stressful, and make sure you have consciously created a support system. *International teacher*

Bring a core set of homely items. Even if you just bring a box of photos in frames, it immediately makes a home when you move somewhere. *Danny and Adele, teaching couple*

Do some research on the school before your move, but perhaps be prepared to go somewhere initially so that you gain experience. Then after the initial contract you can move onto a better school. There is lots to learn from every school and it all helps to build a wealth of collective and memorable experiences. *Jennie and Peter, international teaching couple*

Go for it. I am always happy to learn new things and improve my knowledge and abilities. I think that's important for someone who wants to live abroad, as there is lots of change all the time. *Esther, international teacher*

Take that leap of faith! It is daunting and at times tough but living in a different culture has been amazing. Our work-life balance has been much better and we have been able to save lots of money. *International teacher*

Don't just trust what the school says about itself. Look at International Schools Review for the experiences of past teachers and try to connect with current members of staff if you can. *Kate, international teacher*

Be open minded and relax. Everything will work out. Bring items you need, like certain sheets, make-up, or products. *Lucinda, trailing spouse*

The feeling [of being] overwhelmed at the start is normal. It won't always feel like an exciting adventure. *Becky, international teacher*

Keep your options open when considering your location. It's more important to find the right school, if you are happy there you will be happy wherever you are in the world! *Lydia, company owner, INTA Education*

Request detailed information and approximations of tax bills, cost of living, medical and dental insurance details, and which items of clothing are hard to find in that country (e.g. black school shoes). *Claire, assistant principal*

Advice for parents moving with children

You will be surprised at the many things you can get in Asian countries and, if not, [they] can be shipped. Amazon, although a little expensive, has everything you can think of. Don't bring too much with you – you don't need furniture! *Esther, international teacher*

My initial priority is always to set up our house/apartment so that our children feel like it is their home. We have always sent shipping with us so we find a place for our furniture and then purchase electrical items. After that, I focus on school and try to understand the different curriculum, policies, and procedures, as well as little things like where I can get coffee and how to use the photocopier! My next focus is usually friendships for myself and my children

– we invite people over or to go out somewhere. *Clare, assistant principal*

We tried to make life 'normal', e.g., found swimming lessons our daughter could go to at the weekend, as this was something she was doing at home before we moved. *Becky, international teacher*

Find your clan, and lean on them when you need them. Don't do it alone. Don't fret too much, things work themselves out. Make sure you make time for family calls back home, [and] keep kids involved in family occasions. *Alexandra, trailing spouse*

Sometimes insecurities or difficulties with the transition come out when you least expect them. Even if it appears your child has made a seamless transition, keep inviting them to talk about their feelings. *Kate, international teacher*

There are a number of expat groups for families available. Definitely get involved with these; I've made some good friends by doing this. Consider the age of the child when you move, as this may affect how easy it is. When children are older it may be more difficult for them. *International teacher*

Do lots of research! What school will they go to and what is it like? What can they do in their free time? Can they continue any hobbies that they are passionate about? How often will they be able to see their close family? Will they be safe to go out alone or will you have to take them everywhere? *Trailing spouse*

APPENDIX A

Research Methods

To gather data and feedback for this guide, I used a multi-method approach. By using group responses, interviews, and questionnaires, I varied my sources so I could obtain a fairly diverse sample within my research. I have no affiliations whatsoever with any of the companies I mention.

1. My first approach was to formulate questions to share on Facebook groups for international teaching and relocations (listed in Appendix B). This was a more general approach to ascertain what was of importance to international teachers. The research questions included, but were not limited to, the preferred international teacher recruitment portals, what factors contributed to teachers feeling settled, and also experiences of interviews. I collated the responses and looked for common themes and patterns.

2. I shared the text, chapter by chapter, with current and previous colleagues, Headteachers, and recruiters. They added valuable insights and perspectives to the guide.

3. I held conversations (or mini-interviews) with colleagues to ascertain their experiences of international teaching, as well as for the purposes of researching new angles for this text.

4. I created questionnaires that were sent out to 30 participants: new international teachers, teachers, Headteachers and managers in charge of recruitment. Twenty questionnaires were returned. The questionnaires encouraged each

participant to share their own story, using prompts and open-ended questions.

5. Finally, the guide was sent to peer readers who further digested the work in its entirety and offered their suggestions.

APPENDIX B

Helpful Online Resources for International Teachers and Expats

International teacher/expat groups on Facebook

New to International School Teachers
My group was specifically set up to provide information for teachers considering working abroad. This is a small, supportive group with strict rules on respect for participants. Any questions raised from this guide can be posted here and I will respond. Lists jobs, articles, and recruiters, and provides answers to questions.

International school teachers.
Well established, very large group. Lists jobs, questions around international teaching, articles, Professional Development courses, and teaching aids.

International school teachers
This group is also well established and was created to encourage the flow of information and ideas. It has a similar function to *International school teachers.* group.

Teachers on the Move with Children
A smaller group but with a specific focus. Covers similar areas to the other groups mentioned.

Expatriate teachers - Gulf and the Middle East
A small group focusing on a specific geographical area. Supports mostly job postings.

Teachers in Taiwan
A small group focusing on a specific geographical area. Supports mostly job postings.

Two Fat Expats
A huge group with a wealth of information about different countries, discussions of jobs, and also the roles of dependents such as trailing spouses.

Expat and International School Educators – Financial Advice
A group covering the specifics for saving as an expat. Andrew Hallam often replies and contributes to the site, so you can read his book and ask specific questions.

International delivery of goods

The British Cornershop
This British company offers a huge variety of both fresh and long-life products, delivered to your door, standardly within a week. The delivery charges can be high, depending on where you live.

Next/ASOS/Marks and Spencer
Often big clothes retailers will deliver, so check your favourite shops for their international delivery. In some countries, Next delivers for free.

iHerb.com
Hair, health and personal products delivered directly to your door, at reasonable prices.

Amazon
A huge range of goods; toys, clothes, shoes and books delivered to your doorstep.

Book Depository
A large range of books at reasonable prices delivered worldwide.

Online therapy

Check whether your insurance covers online sessions or in-person sessions in your country of residence.

Getbetterhelp.com supports all kinds of mental health issues, including depression, stress, and anxiety.

The Truman group offer expat-focused psychological care.

APPENDIX C

Third Culture (Expat) Children

Below are recommendations for further reading:

Web

Third Culture Kids/Global Nomads - Lewis & Clark – this website provides many resources including articles, websites, and contacts for support on Third Culture Kids.

Thirdculturekidglobal.com – aimed at building a community; includes personal stories.

Gov.uk - details on how to apply for citizenship in the UK if you have a British parent (born on or after 1 July 2006).

Texts

Third Culture Kids: Growing Up Among Worlds (2009) by David C. Pollock and Ruth E. Van Reken.

Raising Up a Generation of Healthy Third Culture Kids: A Practical Guide to Preventive Care (2020) by Lauren Wells.

Article

Fail, Helen, et al. "Belonging, Identity and Third Culture Kids: Life Histories of Former International School Students." Journal of Research in International Education, vol. 3, no. 3, Dec. 2004, pp. 319–338.

BIBLIOGRAPHY

"Early Childhood Teacher." *Careers.govt.nz.* 1ˢᵗ March 2021, careers. govt.nz/jobs-database/education-and-social-sciences/education/ early-childhood-teacher-kaiako/how-to-enter-the-job.

Hallam, Andrew. *Millionaire Expat.* 2014. New Jersey, John Wiley & Sons, Inc, 2018.

"International College Accreditation." ASIC, 2014-2021. Asickuk. com/college-accreditation/.

Kurtuy, Andrew. "How to write an ATS Resume" *novoresume,* 2019, novoresume.com/career-blog/ats-resume.

Lansing, Jade. "Everything You Need to Know Before Teaching in Dubai" *GoAbroad.com*, 15 Sept. 2020, goabroad.com/articles/ teach-abroad/teaching-in-dubai.

MacDonald, James. "The International School Industry: Examining International Schools through an Economic Lens." *Journal of Research in International Education*, vol. 5, no. 2, Aug. 2006, pp. 191–213, journals.sagepub.com/doi/10.1177/1475240906065618. Accessed 28th December 2020.

Savva, Maria. "Characteristics of the International Educator and the Strategic Role of Critical Incidents." *Journal of Research in International Education*, vol. 14, no. 1, Apr. 2015, pp. 16–28, journals.sagepub.com/doi/abs/10.1177/1475240915570548. Accessed 5th January 2021.

Scarborough, William. "For-Profit and Non-Profit Schools: A View from Singapore American School." *The International Educator (TIE Online)*, 19 Feb. 2015, tieonline.com/article/1536/for-profit-and-non-profit-schools-a-view-from-singapore-american-school.

ACKNOWLEDGMENTS

Firstly, I would like to give a huge thank you to my copy-editor and friend, Helen Gamble. When I first discussed the project with her, she was full of enthusiasm which instilled in me the confidence to have a go at this project. She has been a delight to work with, providing insightful knowledge as a spouse of an international teacher, as well as her incredibly professional service as a freelance editor.

Secondly, I really want to thank my international teacher friends, who tirelessly read through my chapters whilst in production. Those who chose to remain anonymous know who they are, but those I can name are Michael Gallagher, Clare Doyle, Emma Crofts, Val Awad, Stephanie Cantrell, Jennie Bonnalie, and Kristie Funnekotter. I cannot express just how much your support has meant to me. Also, my fabulous peer readers who agreed to read the entire text at the end of term: Michael, Clare, Kristie (again), Keith Gosling, Rowena Bracken, Becky Massey, Jo Connelly, and Lizzie Bottomley-Chang. You all helped to develop this guide with your feedback. Every single piece of advice improved my book a little bit more.

Finally, to all those ex-colleagues, colleagues, colleagues-to-be (that's you Gemma Farr), and spouses who took the time to fill in my detailed questionnaire, I am absolutely bowled over with your honesty and willingness to support other new teachers with your advice. I love how the last chapter was wholly co-created with you, as I feel your voices are so important and may well influence many of those hesitant to relocate.

Thank you, thank you, thank you.

ABOUT THE AUTHOR

 After struggling to establish a work-life balance, and frustrated by the poor working conditions for teachers in the UK, Jess decided to teach abroad. Seeking adventure, she travelled with her husband to Egypt with little more than a backpack and no idea what would happen next. The move was a fortunate one, as she was instantly inspired by all she experienced: the international school offered wonderful facilities and provided abundant resources, there was freedom and flexibility within the curriculum, and moreover, she got to teach well-behaved, curious children.

That first experience, in 2009, was the beginning of a life-long career, where she developed a passion for working internationally. Now an experienced educator, her aim is to provide insight into the world of international teaching, in the hope of inspiring others to have the confidence to change their lives.

She currently lives in Taiwan with her husband, also a teacher, her six year-old daughter, and a fairly new hamster baby. Jess loves to read, travel, explore, and share new experiences with friends and family.

Made in the USA
Columbia, SC
02 August 2021

42842671R00085